THE POETICAL WORKS OF GEORGE HERBERT HERBERT AND CHRISTOPHER HARVEY

Publisher's Note

-:- -:- -:- -:- -:- -:- -:- -:-

THE TEMPLE. THE DEDICATION.

Lord, ray first fruits present themselves to thee;
Yet not mine neither; for from thee they came,
And must return. Accept of them and me,
And make us strive, who shall sing best thy Name.
Turn their eyes hither, who shall make a gain:
Theirs, who shall hurt themselves or me, refrain.

THE CHURCH PORCH.

PEKIKRHASTERIUM.

1. Thou, whose sweet youth and early hopes enhance
Thy rate and price, and mark thee for a treasure,
Hearken unto a Verscr, who may chance
Rhyme thee to good, and make a bait of pleasure:
    A verse may find him, who a Sermon flics,
    And turn delight into a Sacrifice.
2. Beware of lust; it doth pollute and foul
    Whom God in Baptism wash'd with his own blood:
    It blots the lesson written in thy soul;
    The holy lines cannot be understood.
How dare those eyes upon a Bible look,
Much less towards God, whose lust is all their book!
3. Wholly abstain, or wed. Thy bounteous Lord
    Allows thee choice of paths: take no by-ways;
    But gladly weleome what he doth afford;
    Not grudging, that thy lust hath bounds and stays.
Continence hath his joy: weigh both; and so
If rottenness have more, let heaven go.
4. If God had laid all common, certainly
    Man would have been th' encloscr;

out since now
    God hath impaled us, on the contrary
    Man breaks the fence, and every ground will plough. 0 what were man, might he himself misplace! Sure to be cross he would shift feet and face.
5. Drink not the third glass, which thou canst not tame,
When once it is within thee; but before
May'st rule it, as thou list: and pour the shame
Which it would pour on thee, upon the floor.
It is most just to throw that on the ground,
Which would throw me there, if I keep the round.
6. He that is drunken may his mother kill
    Big with his sister: he hath lost the reins,
    Is outlaw'd by himself: all kind of ill
    Did with his liquor slide into his veins.
    The drunkard forfeits Man, and doth divest
All worldly right, save what he hath by beast.
7. Shall I, to please another's wine-sprung mind,
Lose all mine own? God hath given me a measure
Short of his can, and body; must I find
A pain in that, wherein he finds a pleasure?
Stay at the third glass: if thou lose thy hold,
Then thou art modest, and the wine grows bold.
8. If reason move not Gallants, quit the room
(All in a shipwreck shift their several way);
Let not a common ruin thee entomb:
Be not a beast in courtesy, but stay,
    Stay at the third cup, or forego the place.
    Wine above all things doth God's stamp deface.
9. Yet, if thou sin in wine or wanton-

ness,

Boast not thereof; nor make thy shame thy glory.

Frailty gets pardon by submissiveness;

But he that boasts, shuts that out of his story: lie makes flat war with God, and doth defy, With his poor clod of earth the spacious sky.

10 Take not His name, who made thy mouth, in vain:

It gets thee nothing, and hath no excuse.

Lust and wine plead a pleasure, avarice gain: *gain*

But the cheap swearer through his open sluice

Lets his soul run for nought, as little fearing:

Were I an *Epicure,* I could bate swearing.

11 When thou dost tell another's jest, therein

Omit the oaths, which true wit cannot need:

Pick out of tales the mirth, but not the sin.

He lie pares his apple that will cleanly feed.

Play not away the virtue of that name,

Which is thy best stake, when griefs make thee tame.

12 The cheapest sins most dearly punish'd arc;

Because to shun them also is so cheap:

For we have wit to mark them, and to spare.

0 crumble not away thy soul's fair heap.

If thou wilt die, the gates of hell arc broad:

Pride and full sius have made the way a road.

13 Lie not; but let thy heart be true to God,

Thy mouth to it, thy actions to them both:

Cowards tell lies, and those that fear the rod;

The stormy working soul spits lies and froth.

Dare to be true. Nothing can need a lie:

A fault, which needs it most, grows two thereby.

14 Fly idleness, which yet thou canst not fly

By dressing, mistressing, and comple-ment.

If those take up thy day, the Sun will cry Against thee; for his light was only lent.

God gave thy soul brave wings; put not those feathers

Into a bed, to sleep out all ill weathers.

15 Art thou a Magistrate? then be severe:

If studious; copy fair what time hath blurr'd;

Redeem truth from his jaws: if Soldier, Chase brave employments with a naked sword

Throughout the world. Fool not; for all may have,

If they dare try, a glorious life, or grave.

16 0 England! full of sin, but most of sloth!

Spit out thy phlegm, and fill thy breast with glory:

Thy Gentry bleats, as if thy native cloth _

Transfused a shecpishness into thy story:

Not that they all arc so; but that the most Arc gone to grass, and in the pasture lost.

17 This loss springs chiefly from our education.

Some till their ground, but let weeds choke their son:

Some mark a partridge, never their child's fashion: -

Some ship them over, and the thing is done.

Study this art, make it thy great design;

And if God's image move thee not, let thine.

18 Some great estates provide, but do not breed

A mastering mind; so both are lost thereby:

Or else they breed them tender, make them need *flat*

All that they leave; this is Hat poverty.

For he, that needs five thousand pound to live,

Is full as poor as he that needs but five.

19 The way to make thy son rich, is to fill

His mind with rest, before his trunk with riches:

For wealth without contentment, climbs a hill,

To feel those tempests, which fly over ditches.

But if thy son can make ten pound his measure,

Then all thou addest may be call'd his treasure.

20 When thou dost purpose ought (within thy power),

Be sure to do it, though it be but small:

Constancy knits the bones, and makes us stour,

When wanton pleasures beckon us to thrall.

Who breaks his own bond, forfcitcth himself:

What nature made a ship, he makes a shelf.

21 Do all things like a man, not sneakingly:

Think the king sees thee still; for his King does.

Simpering is but a Lay-hypocrisy:

Give it a corner, and the clue undoes.

Who fears to do ill, sets himself to task:

Who fears to do well, sure should wear a mask. '?

22 Look to thy mouth: diseases enter there.

Thou hast two sconces, if thy stomach call;

Carve, or discourse; do not a famine fear.

Who carves, is kind to two; who talks, to all.

Look on meat, think it dirt, then eat a bit;

And say withal, *Earth to earth I commit.*

23 Slight those who say amidst their sickly healths, Thou livest by rule. What cloth not so but man? Houses arc built by rule, and commonwealths. Entice the trusty sun, if that you can,

From his Ecliptic line; beckon the sky.

Who lives by rule, then, keeps good company.

24 Who keeps no guard upon himself, is slack,

And rots to nothing at the next great thaw.

Man is a shop of rules, a wcll-truss'd pack,

Whose every parcel underwrites a law.

Lose not thyself, nor give thy humours way:

God gave them to thee under lock and key.

25 By all means use sometimes to be alone.

Salute thyself: see what thy soul doth wear.

Dare to look in thy chest; for 'tis thine own:

And tumble up and down what thou fmd'st there.

Who cannot rest till he good fellows find,

He breaks up house, turns out of doors his mind.

26 Be thrifty, but not covetous: therefore give

Thy need, thine honour, and thy friend his due.

Never was scraper brave man. Get to live;

Then live, and use it: else, it is not true

That thou hast gotten. Surely use alone

Makes money not a contemptible stone.

27 Never exceed thy income. Youth may make

Even with the year: but age, if it will hit,

Shoots a bow short, and lessens still his stake,

As the day lessens, and his life with it.

Thy children, kindred, friends upon thee call;

Before thy journey fairly part with all.

28 Yet in thy thriving still misdoubt some evil;

Lest gaining gain on thee, and make thee dim

To all things else. Wealth is the conjurer's devil;

Whom when he thinks he hath, the devil hath him.

Gold thou may'st safely touch; but if it stick

Unto thy hands, it woundcth to the quick.

29 What skills it, if a bag of stones or gold

About thy neck do drown thee? raise thy head;

Take stars for money; stars not to be told

By any art, yet to be purchased.

None is so wasteful as the scraping dame:

She loscth three for one; her soul, rest, fame.

30 By no means run in debt: take thine own measure.

AVho cannot live on twenty pound a year,

Cannot on forty: he's a man of pleasure,

A kind of Miing that's for itself too dear.

The curious unthrift makes his clothes too wide,7

And spares himself, but would his tailor chide.

31 Spend not on hopes. They that by pleading clothes

Do fortunes seek, when worth and service fail,

Would have their tale believed for their oaths,

And are like empty vessels under sail.

Old courtiers know this; therefore set out so,

As all the day thou may'st hold out to go.

32 In clothes, cheap handsomeness doth bear the bell.

Wisdom's a trimmer thing than shop e'er gave.

Say not then, This with that lace will do well;

But, This with my discretion will be brave.

Much curiousness is u perpetual wooing.

Nothing with labour, folly long a doing.

33 Play not for gain, but sport. Who plays for more

Than he can lose with pleasure, stakes his heart:

Perhaps his wife's too, and whom shc hath bore:

Servants and churches also play their part.

Only a herald, who that way doth pass,

Finds his crack'd name at length in the Church-glass.

34 If yet thou love game at so dear a rate,

Learn this, that hath old gamesters dearly cost:

Dost lose? rise up; dost win? rise in that state.

Who strive to sit out losing hands, arc lost.

Game is a civil gunpowder, in peace

Blowing up houses with their whole increase.

35 In Conversation boldness now bears sway.

But know, that nothing can so foolish be,

As empty boldness: therefore first assay

To stinT thy mind with solid bravery;

Then march on gallant: get substantial worth: Boldness gilds finely, and will set it forth.

36 Be sweet to all. Is thy complexion sour?

Then keep such company; make them thy allay:

Get a sharp wife, a servant that will lour.

A stumbler stumbles least in rugged way.

Command thyself in chief. He life's war knows,

Whom all his passions follow, as he goes.

Catch not at quarrels. lie that dares not speak

Plainly and home, is coward of the two.

Think not thy fame at every twitch will break:

By great deeds show, that thou canst little do;

And do them not: that shall thy wisdom be;

And change thy temperance into bravery.

If that thy fame with every toy be posed,

Tis a thin web, which poisonous fancies make;

But the great soldier's honour was composed

Of thicker stuff, which would endure a shake.

Wisdom picks friends; civility plays the rest.

A toy shunn'd cleanly passcth with the best.

Laugh not too much: the witty man laughs least:

For wit is news only to ignorance.

Less at thine own things laugh; lest in the jest

Thy person share, and the conceit advance.

Make not thy sport, abuses: for the fly,

That feeds on dung, is coloured thereby.

Pick out of mirth, like stones out of thy ground, "rofaneness, filthiness, abusiveness.

Those arc the scum, with which coarse wits abound:

The fine may spare these well, yet not go less.

All things arc big with jest: nothing that's plain

But may be witty, if thou hast the vein.

Wit's an unruly engine, wildly striking

Sometimes a friend, sometimes the engineer:

Hast thou the knack / pamper it not with liking:

But if thou want it, buy it not too dear.

Many affecting wit beyond their power,

Have got to be a dear fool for an hour.

A sad wise valour is the brave complexion,

That leads the van, and swallows up the cities.

The giggler is a milk-maid, whom infection,

Or a fired beacon frightcth from his ditties.

Then he's the sport: the mirth then in him rests,

And the sad man is cock of all his jests.

Towards great persons use respective boldness:

That temper gives them theirs, and yet doth take

Nothing from thine: in service, care, or coldness,

Doth ratably thy fortunes mar or make.

Feed no man in his sins: for adulation

Doth make thee parcel-devil in damnation.

Envy not greatness: for thou makest thereby

Thyself the worse, and so the distance greater.

Be not thine own worm: yet such jealousy,

As hurts not others, but may make thcc better,

Is a good spur. Correct thy passion's spite;

Then may the beasts draw thee to happy light.

When baseness is exalted, do not bate

The place its honour for the person's sake.

The shrine is that which thou dost venerate;

And not the beast, that bears it on his back.

I care not though the cloth of State should be -)(.

Not of rich arras, but mean tapestry.

Thy friend put in thy bosom: wear his eyes

Still in thy heart, that he may see what's there.

If cause require, thou art his sacrifice;

Thy drops of blood must pay down all his fear;

But love is lost; the way of friendship's gone;

Though David had his Jonathan, Christ his John.

Yet be not surety, if thou be a father.

Love is a personal debt. I cannot give

My children's right, nor ought he take it: rather

Both friends should die, than hinder them to live.

Fathers first enter bonds to nature's cnds;

And arc her sureties, ere they are a friend's.

If thou be single, all thy goods and ground

Submit to love; but yet not more than all.

Give one estate, as one life. None is bound

To work for two, who brought himself to t'rall.

God made me one man; love makes me no more,

Till labour come, and make my weakness score.

In thy Discourse, if thou desire to please:

All such is courteous, useful, new, or witty:

Usefulness comes by labour, wit by ease;

Courtesy grows in court; news in the city.

Get a good stock of these, then draw the card

That suits him best, of whom thy speech is heard.

Entice all neatly to what they know best;

For so thou dost thyself and him a pleasure: (But a proud ignorance will lose his rest,

Rather than show his cards), steal from his treasure

What to ask further. Doubts well-raised do lock

The speaker to thee, and preserve thy stock.

If thou be Master-gunner, spend not all

That thou canst speak, at once; but husband it,

And give men turns of speech: do not forestall

By lavishness thine own, and others' wit,

As if thou madest thy will. A civil guest

Will no more talk all, than cat all the feast.

Be calm in arguing: for fierceness makes

Error a fault, and truth discourtesy.

Why should I feel another man's mistakes

More, than his sicknesses or poverty /

In love I should: but anger is not love,

Nor wisdom neither; therefore gently move.

Calmness is great advantage: he that lets

Another chafe, may warm him at his fire:

Mark all his wanderings, and enjoy his frets;

As cunning fencers suffer heat to tire.

Truth dwells not in the clouds: the bow that's thero

Doth often aim at, never hit, the sphere.

Mark what another says: for many arc

Full of themselves, and answer their own notion.

Take all into thee; then with equal care

Balance each dram of reason, like a potion.

If truth be with thy friend, be with them both:

Share in the conquest, and confess a troth.

Be useful where thou livest, that they may

Both want, and wish thy pleasing presenco still.

Kindness, good parts, great places arc the way
To compass this. Find out men's wants and will,
And meet them there. All worldly joys go lesa
To the one joy of doing kindnesses.
Pitch thy behaviour low, thy projects high;
So shalt thou humble and magnanimous be:
Sink not in spirit: who aimeth at the sky
Shoots higher much than he that means a tree.
A grain of glory mixt with humbleness
Cures both a fever and lethargickness.
Let thy mind still be bent, still plotting where,
And when, and how the business may be done.
Slackness breeds worms; but the sure traveller,
Though he alight sometimes, still goeth on.
Active and stirring spirits live alone:
Write on the others, *Here lies such a one.*
Slight not the smallest loss, whether it bo
In love or honour; take account of all:
Shine like the sun in every corner: see
Whether thy stock of credit swell, or fall.
Who say, / *care not,* those I give for lost;
And to instruct them, 'twill not quit the cost.
Scorn no man's love, though of a mean degree (Love is a present for a mighty king);
Much less make any one thine enemy.
As guns destroy, so may a little sling.
The cunning workman never doth refuse
The meanest tool, that he may chance to use.
All foreign wisdom doth amount to this,
To take all that is given; whether wealth,
Or love, or language; nothing comes amiss:

A good digestion tumeth all to health:
And then as far as fair behaviour may,
Strike off all scores; none are so clear as they.
Keep all thy native good, and naturalize
All foreign of that name; but scorn their ill:
Embrace their activeness, not vanities.
Who follows all things, forfeitcth his will.
If thou obscrvest strangers in each it,
In time they'll run thee out of all thy wit.
Affect in things about thee cleanliness,
That all may gladly board thee, as a flower.
Slovens take up their stock of noisomeness
Beforehand, and anticipate their last hour.
Let thy mind's sweetness have his operation
Upon thy body, clothes, and habitation.
v.

Iii Alms regard thy means, and others' merit.
Think heaven a better bargain, than to give
Only thy single market-money for it.
Join hands with God to make a man to live.
Give to all, something; to a good poor man,
Till thou change names, and be where he began.
Man is God's image; but a poor man is
Christ's stamp to boot: both images regard.
God reckons for him, counts the favour his:
Write, *So much given to God;* thou shalt be heard.
Let thy alms go before, and keep heaven's gate
Open for thee; or both may come too late.
Restore to God his due in tithe and time:
A tithe purloin'd cankers the whole estate.
Sundays observe: think when the bells

do chime,
'Tis angels' music; therefore come not late.
God then deals blessings: if a King did so,
Who would not haste, nay give, to see the show?
Twice on the day his due is understood;
For all the week thy food so oft he gave thee.
Thy cheer is mended; bate not of the food,
Because 'tis better, and perhaps may save thee.
Thwart not th' Almighty God: 0 be not cross.
Fast when thou wilt; but then 'tis gain, not loss.
Though private prayer be a brave design,
Yet public hath more promises, more love:
And love's a weight to hearts, to eyes a sign.
We all are but cold suitors; let us move
Where it is wannest. Leave thy six and seven;
Pray with the most: for where most pray, is heaven. When once thy foot enters the Church, be bare. God is more there, than thou: for thou art there Only by his permission. Then beware, And make thyself all reverence and fear. jy Kneeling ne'er spoil'd silk stocking: quit thy state. All equal arc within the Church's gate.
Resort to sermons, but to prayers most: Praying's the end of preaching. 0 be drest; Stay not for th' other pin: why thou hast lost A joy for it worth worlds. Thus hell doth jest Away thy blessings, and extremely flout thee,
Thy clothes being fast, but thy soul loose about thco.
In time of service seal up both thine eyes,
And send them to thy heart; that spying sin,
They may weep out the stains by them did rise:
Those doors being shut, all by the car comes in.
Who marks in church-time others' symmetry,

Makes all their beauty his deformity.

Let vain or busy thoughts have there no part:

Bring not thy plough, thy plots, thy pleasures thither.

Christ purged his temple; so must thou thy heart.

All worldly thoughts are but thieves met together

To cozen thee. Look to thy actions well;

For Churches cither arc our heaven or hell.

Judge not the preacher; for he is thy Judge:

If thou mislikc him, thou conccivest him not.

God calleth preaching folly. Do not grudge

To pick out treasures from an earthen pot.

The worst speak something good.: if all want sense,

God takes a text, and prcachcth patience.

B 7f

He that gets patience, and the blessing which

Preachers conclude with, hath not lost his pains.

lie that by being at Church escapes the ditch,

"Which he might fall in by companions, gains.

He that loves God's abode, and to combine

With saints on earth, shall one day with them shine.

Jest not at preachers' language, or expression:

How know'st thou, but thy sins made him miscarry?

Then turn thy faults and his into confession:

God sent him, whatsoe'er he be: 0 tarry,

And love him for his Master: his condition,

Though it be ill, makes him no ill Physician.

None shall in hell such bitter pangs endure

As those, who mock at God's way of salvation.

Whom oil and balsams kill, what salve can cure?

They drink with greediness a full damnation.

The Jews refused thunder; and we, folly.

Though God do hedge us in, yet who is holy?

Sum up at night, what thou hast done by day;

And in the morning, what thou hast to do.

Dress and undress thy soul: mark the decay C

And growth of it: if with thy watch, that too

Be down, then wind up both; since we shall bo

Most surely judged, make thy accounts agree.

In brief, acquit thee bravely; play the man.

Look not on pleasures as they come, but go.

Defer not tho least virtue: life's poor span

Make not an ell, by trifling in thy woe.

If thou do ill, the joy fades, not tho pains:

If well, the pain doth fade, the joy remains.

The cnuRcn.

SUPERLIMlNARE.

Thou, whom the former precepts have
Sprinkled and taught, how to behave
Thyself in Church; approach, and taste
The Church's mystical repast.

Avoid profaneness; come not here:
Nothing but holy, pure, and clear,
Or that which groaneth to be so,
May at his peril further go.

THE ALTAR.

A Broken Altar, Lord, thy servant rears,

Made of a heart, and cemented with tears:

Whose parts are as thy hand did frame;

No workman's tool hath touch'd the same.

A Heart alone
Is such a stone,
As nothing but
Thy power QpthY'ut. /
Wherefore each part
Of my hard heart

Meets in this frame,
To praise thy name:
That, if I chance to hold my peace,
These stones to praise thee may not cease.

0 let thy blessed Sacrifice be mine,
And sanctify this Altar to be thinp.

THE SACRIFICE. *0 all ye, who pass by, whose eyes and mind To worldly things are sharp, but to me blind; To me, who took eyes that I might you find: Was ever grief like mine?*

The Princes of my people make a head

Against their Maker: they do wish me dead,

"Who cannot wish, except I give them bread;
Was ever grief like mine?

Without me each one, who doth now mo brave,

Had to this day been an Egyptian slave.

They use that power against me, which I gave:
Was ever grief like mine f

Mine own Apostle, who the bag did bear,

Though he had all I had, did not forbear

To sell mo also, and to put me there:
Was ever grief like mine?

For thirty pence he did my death devise,

Who at three hundred did the ointment prize,

Not half so sweet as my sweet sacrifice:
Was ever grief like mine?

Therefore my soul melts, and my heart's dear trcasuro Drops blood (the only beads) my words to measure: *0 let this cup pass, if it be thy pleasure: Was ever grief like mine?*

These drops being temper'd with a sinner's tears,

A balsam arc for both the Hemispheres,

Curing all wounds, but mine; all, but my fears.

Was ever grief like mine?

Yet my Disciples sleep: I cannot gain

One hour of watching; but their drowsy brain

Comforts not me, and doth my doctrine stain: *Was ever grief like mine?*

Arise, arise, they come! Look how they run!

Alas! what haste they make to be undone!

How with their lanterns do they seek the sun!
Was ever grief like mine?

With clubs and staves they seek me, as a thief,
Who am the way of truth, the true relief,
Most true to those who arc my greatest grief:
Was ever grief like mine?

Judas, dost thou betray me with a kiss *l*
Canst thou find hell about my lips? and miss
Of life, just at the gates of life and bliss?
Was ever grief like mine?

See, they lay hold on me, not with the hands
Of faith, but fury; yet at their commands
I suffer binding, who have loosed their bands:
Was ever grief like mine f

All my Disciples fly; fear puts a bar
Betwixt my friends and me. They leave the star,
That brought the wise men of the East from far: *Was ever grief like mine?*

Then from one ruler to another bound
They lead me: urging, that it was not sound
What I taught: Comments would the text confound.
Was ever grief like mine t

The Priests and Riders all false witness seek
'Gainst him, who seeks not life, but is the meek
And ready Paschal Lamb of this great week:
Was ever grief like mine?

Then they accuse me of great blasphemy,
That I did thrust into the Deity,
Who never thought that any robbery:
Was ever grief like mine?

Some said, that I the Temple to the floor
In three days razed, and raised as before.
Why, ho that built the world can do much more:
Was ever grief like mine?

Then they condemn me all with that same breath,
Which I do give them daily, unto death.
Thus Adam my first breathing rendereth:

Was ever grief like mine?

They bind, and lead me unto Ilcrod: he
Sends me to Pilate. This makes them agree;
But yet their friendship is my enmity.
Was ever grief like mine?

Ilcrod and all his bands do set me light,
Who teach all hands to war, fingers to fight,
And only am the Lord of hosts and might.
Was ever grief like mine t

Herod in judgment sits, while I do stand;
Examines me with a censorious hand:
I him obej, who all things else command:
Was ever grief like mine?

The Jews accuse me with despitefulness;
And vying malice with my gentleness,
Pick quarrels with their only happiness:
Was ever grief like mine?

I answer nothing, but with patience prove
If stony hearts will melt with gentle love.
But who does hawk at eagles with a dove *l*
Was ever grief like mine?

My silence rather doth augment their cry;
My dove doth back into my bosom fly,
Because the raging waters still arc high:
Was ever grief like mine?

Hark how they cry aloud still, *Crucify:*
It is not fit he live a day, they cry,
Who cannot live less than eternally:
Was cvej' grief like mine?

Pilate a stranger holdeth off; but they,
Mine own dear people, cry, *Away, away,*
With noises confused frighting the day:
Was ever grief like mine?

Yet still they shout, and cry, and stop their ears,
Putting my life among their sins and fears,
And therefore with *my blood on them and theirs* :
Was ever grief like mine?

See how spite cankers things. These words aright
Used, and wish'd, arc tho whole world's light:
But honey is their gall, brightness their night:
Was ever grief like mine?

They choose a murderer, and all agree
In him to do themselves a courtesy;
For it was their own cause who killed me:
Was ever grief like mine?

And a seditious murderer he was:
But I tho Prince of Peace; peace that doth pass
All understanding, more than heaven doth glass: *Was ever grief like mine?*

"Why, Cscsar is their only King, not I:
He clave the stony rock, when thcy were dry;
But surely not their hearts, as I well try: *Was ever grief like mine?*

Ah, how they scourge mo! yet my tenderness Doubles each lash: and yet their bitterness Winds up my grief to a mysteriousness: *Was ever grief like mine?*

They buffet me, and box me as they list,
"Who grasp the earth and heaven with my fist,
And never yet, whom I would punish, miss'd:
Was ever grief like mine?

Behold, they spit on mo in scornful wise;
Who with my spittle gave tho blind man eyes,
Leaving his blindness to mine enemies:
Was *ever grief like mine?*

My face they cover, though it be divine.
As Moses' face was veiled, so is mine,
Lest on their double-dark souls cither shine: *Was ever grief like mine?*

Servants and abjects flout me; they are witty:
Notv prophesy who strikes thee, is their ditty.
So they in me deny themselves all pity:
Was ever grief like mine?

And now I am dcliver'd unto death,
Which each one calls for so with ut-

most breath,

That he before me well-nigh su-flercth: *Was ever grief like mine?*

Weep not, dear friends, since I for both have wept,

When all my tears were blood, the while you slept:

Your tears for your own fortunes should be kept:

Was ever grief like mine?

The soldiers lead me to the common hall;

There they deride me, they abuse me all:

Yet for twelve heavenly legions I could call:

Was ever grief like mine? Then with a scarlet robe they me array; Which shows my blood to be the only way, And cordial left to repair man's decay: *Was ever grief like mine?* Then on my head a crown of thorns I wear; For these are all the grapes Sion doth bear, Though I my viue planted and watcr'd there: IT as *ever grief like mine?*

So sits the earth's great curse in Adam's fall

Upon my head; so I remove it all

From th' earth unto my brows, and bear the thrall:

Was ever grief like mine?

Then with the reed they gave to me before,

They strike my head, the rock from whence all store

Of heavenly blessings issue ever-more: *Was ever grief like mine?*

They bow their knees to me, and cry, *If ail, King:*

Whatever scofTs or scornfulness can bring,

I am the floor, the sink, where they it fling:

Was ever grief like mine?

Yet since man's sceptres arc as frail as reeds, And thoruy all their crowns, bloody their weeds; I, who am Truth, turn into truth their deeds: *Was ever grief like mine ?*

The soldiers also spit upon that face Which Angels did desire to have the grace,

And Prophets once to see, but found no place:

Was ever grief like mine?

Thus trimmed, forth they bring me to the rout,

Who *Crucify him,* cry with one strong shout.

God holds his peace at man, and man cries out:

Was ever grief like mine?

They lead me in once more, and putting then

Mine own clothes on, they lead me out again.

Whom devils fly, thus is he toss'd of men:

Was ever grief like mine?

And now weary of sport, glad to en-gross

All spite in one, counting my life their loss,

They carry me to my most bitter cross: *Was ever grief like mine?*

My cross I bear myself, until I faint: Then Simon bears it for me by con-straint,

The decreed burden of each mortal Saint:

Was ever grief like mine? 0 all ye who pass by, behold and see:

Man stole the fruit, but I must climb the tree;

The tree of life to all, but only me: *Was ever grief like mine f*

Lo, here I hang, charged with a world of sin,

The greater world o' the two; for that came in

By words, but this by sorrow I must win:

Was ever grief like mincf

Such sorrow, as if sinful man could feel,

Or feel his part, he would not cease to kneel,

Till all were melted, though he were all steel.

Was ever grief like mine f

But, *0 my God, my God!* why leavest thou me,

The Son, in whom thou dost delight to be?

My God, my God Never was grief like mine.

Shame tears my soul, my body many a wound; Sharp nails pierce this, but sharper that confound; Reproaches, which arc free, whilo I am bound: *Was*

ever grief like mine? Now heal thyself, Physician; now come down. But now I die; now all is finished.

Alas! I do so, when I left iny crown

And Father's smile for you, to feel his frown:

Was ever grief like mine?

In healing not myself, there doth con-sist

All that salvation, which ye now resist;

Your safety in my sickness doth subsist:

Was ever grief like mine?

Betwixt two thieves I spend my ut-most breath,

As ho that for some robbery suflercth.

Alas! what have I stolen from you? death:

Was ever grief like mine?

A king my title is, prcfix'd on high;

Yet by my subjects I'm condemn'd to die

A servile death in servile company:

Was ever grief like mine?

They gave me vinegar mingled with gall,

But more with malice: yet, when they did call,

With Manna, Angels' food, I fed them all: *Was ever grief like mine?*

They part my garments, and by lot dispose

My coat, the type of love, which once cured those

Who sought for help, never malicious foes: *Was ever grief like mine t*

Nay, after death their spito shall fur-ther go;

For they will pierce my side, I full well know;

That as sin came, so Sacraments might flow:

Was ever grief like mine t

My woe, man's weal: and now I bow my head:

Only let others say, when I am dead, *Never was grief like mine.* THE THANKS-GIVING.

0 King of grief! (a title strange, yet true, To thee of all kings only duo) 0 King of wounds! how shall I grieve for thee,

Who in all grief preventest me *l* Shall I weep blood *l* why, thou hast wept such store, That all thy body was one door.

Shall I be scourged, flouted, boxed, sold

1

'Tis but to tell the tale is told.
My God, my God, why dost thou part from me?
Was such a grief as cannot be.
Shall I then sing, skipping, thy doleful story,
And side with thy triumphant glory?
Shall thy strokes be my stroking / thorns, my flower?
 Thy rod, my posic? cross, my bower / But how then shall I imitate thee, and
 Copy thy fair, though bloody hand / Surely I will revenge me on thy love,
And try who shall victorious prove.
If thou dost give me wealth; I will restore
All back unto thee by the poor.
If thou dost give mo honour; men shall see,
 The honour doth belong to thee.
1 will not marry; or, if she be mine,
 She and her children shall be thine.
My bosom-friend, if he blaspheme thy name, I will tear thence his love and fame. One half of me being gone, the rest I give
 Unto some Chapel, die or live. As for thy passion—but of that anon,
 When with the other I have done. For thy predestination, I'll contrive,
 That three years hence, if I survive,
I'll build a spital, or mend common ways,
 But mend my own without delays.
Then I will use the works of thy creation,
 As if I used them but for fashion. The world and I will quarrel; and the year
 Shall not perceive, that I am here. My music shall find thee, and every string
 Shall have his attribute to sing; That altogether may accord in thee,
 And prove one God, one harmony. If thou shalt give mo wit, it shall appear,
 If thou hast given it me, 'tis here. Nay, I will read thy book, and never move
 Till I have found therein thy love;
Thy art of love, which I'll turn back on thee, 0 my dear Saviour, Victory! Then for thy passion—I will do for that—
 Alas! my God, I know not what.

THE REPRISAL.

I Have consider'd it, and find There is
no dealing with thy mighty passion For though I die for thee, I am behind;
 My sins deserve the condemnation.
0 make me innocent, that I
May give a disentangled state and free;
And yet thy wounds still my attempts defy,
For by thy death I die for thee.
Ah! was it not enough that thou
By thy eternal glory didst outgo me?
Could'st thou not grief's sad conquests me allow,
But in all victories overthrow me / Yet by confession will I come
Into the conquest. Though I can do nought
Against thee, in thee I will overcome
 The man, who once against thee fought.

 ' THE AGONY.

Philosophers have measured mountains,
Fathom'd the depths of seas, of states, and kings,
Walk'd with a staff to heaven, and traced fountains;
But there arc two vast, spacious things,
The which to measure it doth more behove:
Yet few there arc that sound them; Sin and Love.
Who would know Sin, let him repair
Unto Mount Olivet; there shall he see
A.man, so wrung with pains, that all his hair,
His skin, his garments, bloody be. *tf*
Sin is that Press and Vice, which forceth pain
To hunt his cruel food through every vein.
Who knows not Love, let him assay,
And taste that juice, which on the cross a pike
Did set again abroach; then let him say
If ever he did taste the like.
Love is that liquor sweet and most divine,
Which my God feels as blood; but I, as wine.

THE SINNER.

Lord, how I am all ague, when I seek
 What I have treasured in my memory!
Since, if my soul make even with the week,
 Each seventh note by right is due to
thee.
 I find there quarries of piled vanities,
 But shreds of holiness, that dare not venturo
To show their face, since cross to thy decrees:
 There the circumference earth is, heaven the centre.
 In so much dregs the quintessence is small:
The spirit and good extract of my heart
Comes to about the many hundredth part.
 Yet, Lord, restore thine image, hear my call:
 And though my hard heart scarce to thee can groan,? (Remember that thou once didst write in stone.

GOOD FRIDAY. 0 MY chief good, How shall I measure out thy blood? How shall 1 count what thee befell,
And each grief tclH
 Shall I thy woes Number according to thy foes? Or, since one star show'd thy first breath,
 Shall all thy death?
Or shall each leaf,
Which falls in Autumn, score a-grief?
Or cannot leaves, but fruit, be sign,
Of the true vine?
Then let each hour
Of my whole life one grief devour;
That thy distress through all may run,
And be my sun.
Or rather let
My several sins their sorrows get;
That, as each beast his cure doth know,
Each sin may so.
 Since blood is fittest, Lord, to write
Thy sorrows in, and bloody fight;
My heart hath store; write there, where in
One box doth lie both ink and sin:
c
 That when Sin spies so many foes,
Thy whips, thy nails, thy wounds, thy woes,
All come to lodge there, Sin may say,
No room for me, and fly away.
 Sin being gone, 0 fill the place,
And keep possession with thy grace;
Lest sin take courage and return,
And all the writings blot or burn.

REDEMPTION.

 Having been tenant long to a rich

Lord,

Not thriving, I resolved to be bold,
And make a suit unto him, to afford
A new small-rented lease, and cancel th' old.

In Heaven at his manor I him sought:
They told me there, that he was lately gone
About some land, which he had dearly bought
Long since on earth, to take possession.

I straight return'd, and knowing his great birth,
Sought him accordingly in great resorts;
In cities, theatres, gardens, parks, and courts:
At length I heard a ragged noise and mirth
Of thieves and murderers: there I him espied,
Who straight, *Your suit is granted,* said, and died.

SEPULCHRE.

0 Blessed body! whither art thou thrown? No lodging for thee, but a cold hard stone? So many hearts on earth, and yet not one
Receive thee?
Sure there is room within our hearts good store;
For they can lodge transgressions by the score:
Thousands of toys dwell there, yet out of door
They leave thee.
But that which shows them large, shows them unfit.
Whatever sin did this pure rock commit,
Which holds thee now? Who hath indited it
Of murder *l*
Where our hard hearts took up of stones to brain thee,
And missing this, most falsely did arraign thee;
Only these stones in quiet entertain thee,
And order.
And as of old, the Law by heavenly art
Was writ in stone; so thou, which also art
The letter of the word, find'st no fit heart

To hold thee.
Yet do wo still persist as we began,
And so should perish, but that nothing can,
Though it bo cold, hard, foul, from loving man
Withhold thee.

EASTER.

Rise, heart; thy Lord is risen. jSingJiis praise Without delays,
Who takes thee by the hand, that thou likewise
Jjl.t_u prK.With him may'st rise:
That, as his death caleined thee to dust,
His life may makethee gold, and much more, Just.

Awake, my lute, and struggle for thy part
With all thy art.
The cross taught all wood to resound his name
Who bore the same,
His stretched sinews taught all strings, what key *J*
Is best to celebrate this most high day. *y y* Consort both heart and lute, and twist a song Pleasant and long:
Or since all music is but three parts vied,
. — And multiplied; 0 let thy blessed Spirit bear a part,
And make up our defects with his sweet art.) (
I Got me flowers to strew thy way;
I got me boughs off many a tree:
But thou wast up by break of day,
And brought'st thy sweets along with thee.
V,.a.»-» iTho Sun arising in the East,
Though he give light, and th' East perfume;
If they should offer to contest
With thy arising, they presume.

EASTER WINGS.

LORD, WHO CREATEDST MAN IN WEALTH AND STORE,
THOUGH FOOLISHLY HE LOST THE SAME,
DECAYING MORE AND MORE, ", TILL HE BECAME
MOST POOR:
WITH THEE OH LET ME RISE ff ....'’" , AS LARKS, HARMONIOUSLY, AND SING THIS DAY THY VICTORIES: THEN SHALL THE FALL FURTHER THE FLIGHT IN ME. MY TENDER AGE IN SORROW DID BEGIN:

AND STILL WITH SICKNESSES AND SHAME
THOU DIDST SO PUNISH SIN, --
THAT I BECAME ,, «/
MOST THIN. WITH THEE
LET ME COMBINE,
AND FEEL THIS DAY THY VICTORY,
FOR, IF I IMP MY WING ON THINE,
AFFLICTION SHALL ADVANCE THE FLIGHT IN ME.

HOLY BAPTISM.

As he that sees a dark and shady grove,
Stays not, but looks beyond it on the sky;
So when I view ray sins, mine eyes remove
More backward still, and to that water fly,
Which is above the heavens, whose spring and vent Is in ray dear Redeemer's pierced side. 0 blessed streams! either ye do prevent
And stop our sins from growing thick and wide,
Or else give tears to drown them, as they grow. In you Redemption measures all my time, And spreads the plaster equal to the crime:
You taught the book of life my name, that so,
Whatever future sins should me miscall,
Your first acquaintance might discredit all.

HOLY BAPTISM.

Since, Lord, to thee
A narrow way and little gate
Is all the passage, on my infancy
Thou didst lay hold, and antedate
My faith in ine.
0 let me still Write thee great God, and me a child:
Let mo be soft and supple to thy will,
Small to myself, to others mild,
Bchithcr ill.
Although by stealth
My flesh get on; yet let her sister
My soul bid nothing, but preserve her wealth:
The growth of flesh is but a blister;
Childhood is health.

NATURE.

Full of rebellion, I would die,
Or fight, or travel, or deny
That thou hast aught to do with me.

0 tame my heart; It is thy highest art To captivate strong holds to thee.

If thou shalt let this venom lurk,
And in suggestions fume and work,
My soul will turn to bubbles straight,
And thence by kind
Vanish into a wind,
Making thy workmanship deceit.
0 smooth my rugged heart, and there
Engrave thy reverend law and fear;
Or make a new one, since the old
Is sapless grown,
And a much fitter stone
To hide my dust, than thee to hold.

SIN.

Lord, with what care hast thou begirt us round! Parents first season us: then schoolmasters Deliver us to laws; they send us bound
To rules of reason, holy messengers,
Pulpits and Sundays, sorrow dogging sin,
Afflictions sorted, anguish of all sizes.
Fine nets and stratagems to catch us in,
Bibles laid open, millions of surprises,
Blessings beforehand, ties of gratefulness,
The sound of glory ringing in our cars;
Without, our shame; within, our consciences;
Angels and grace, eternal hopes and fears.
. Yet all these fences and their whole array
One cunning bosom-sin blows quite away.

AFFLICTION.

Whek first thou didst entice to thee my heart,
I thought the service brave
So many joys I writ down for my part,
Besides what I might have
Out of my stock of natural delights,
Augmented with thy gracious benefits.
I looked on thy furniture so fine,
And made it fine to me;
Thy glorious household-stuff did me entwine,
And 'tice me unto thee.
Such stars I counted mine: both heaven and earth
Paid me my wages in a world of mirth.

What pleasures could I want, whose King I served,
Where joys my fellows were 1
Thus argued into hopes, my thoughts reserved
No place for grief or fear;
Therefore my sudden soul caught at the place,
And made her youth and fierceness seek thy face:
At first thou gavest me milk and sweetnesses; 1 had my wish and way:
My days were strew'd with flowers and happiness:
There was no month but May. But with my years sorrow did twist and grow, And made a party unawares for woe.
My flesh began unto my soul in pain,
Sicknesses cleave my bones,
Consuming agues dwell in every vein,
And tune my breath to groans:
Sorrow was all my soul; I scarce believed,
Till grief did tell me roundly, that I lived.
When I got health, thou took'st away my life,
And more; for my friends die:
My mirth and edge was lost; a blunted knife
Was of more use than I.
Thus thin and lean, without a fence or friend,
I was blown through with every storm and wind.
Whereas my birtU and spirit rather took
The way that takes the town;
Thou didst betray me to a lingering book,
And wrap me in a gown. 7
I was entangled in the world of strife,
Before I had the power to change my life.
Yet, for I thrcaten'd oft the siege to raise,
Not simpering all mine age,
Thou often didst with Academic praise
Melt and dissolve my rage.
I took thy sweeten'd pill, till I came near;

I could not go away, nor persevere.
Yet lest perchance I should too happy be In my unhappiness,
Turning my purge to food, thou throwest me
Into more sicknesses.
Thus doth thy power cross-bias me, not making
Thine own gift good, yet me from my ways taking.
Now I am here, what thou wilt do with me
None of my books will show:
I read, and sigh, and wish I were a tree;
For sure then I should grow
To fruit or shade: at least some bird would trust
Her household to me, and I should be just.
Yet, though thou troublest me, I must be meek;
In weakness must be stout. Well, I will change the service, and go seek
Somo other Master out. Ah,'my dear God! though I am clean forgot, Let me not love thee, if I love thee not.

V REPENTANCE.

Lokd, I confess my sin is great;
Great is my sin. Oh! gently treat With thy quick flower, thy momentary bloom;
Whose life still pressing _V-Is one undressing,
A steady aiming at a tomb.
Man's age is two hours' work, or three;
Each day doth round about us see.
Thus arc wc to delights: but we arc all
To sorrows old,
If life bo told
From what life feeleth, Adam's fall.
0 let thy height of mercy then
Compassionate short-breathed men,
Cut mc not off' for my most foul transgression:
I do confess My foolishness;
My God, accept of my confession.
Sweeten at length this bitter bowl,
Which thou hast pour'd into my soul;
Thy wormwood turn to health, winds to fair weather
For if thou stay,
I and this day,
As wc did rise, wc die together.
When thou for sin rebukest man,

Forthwith ho waxcth woo and wan: Bitterness fills our bowels; all our hearts
 Pine, and decay, And drop away,
And carry with them th' other parts.

 But thou wilt sin and grief destroy;
That so the broken bones may joy,
And tune together in a well-set song,
Full of his praises
Who dead men raises.

 Fractures well cured make us more strong.

FAITH.

Lord, how couldst thou so much appease Thy wrath for sin, as, when man's sight was dim, And could see little, to regard his ease,
 And bring by Faith all things to him
"i Hungry I was, and had no meat:
I did conceit a most delicious feast;
I had it straight, and did as truly cat,
 As ever did a weleome guest.

 There is a rare outlandish root, Which when I could not get, I thought it here:
That apprehension cured so well my foot,
 That I can walk to heaven well near.

 I owed thousands and much more: I did believe that I did nothing owe, And lived accordingly; my creditor
 Believes so too, and lets me go.

 Faith makes me anything, or all That I believe is in the sacred story: And when sin placcth me in Adam's fall,
 Faith sets me higher in his glory.

If I go lower in the book,
What can bo lower than the common manger?
Faith puts me there with Him, who sweetly took
Our flesh and frailty, death and danger.
If bliss had lien in art or strength,
None but the wise and strong had gained it:
Where now by Faith all arms are of a length;
One size doth all conditions fit.

 A peasant may believe as much As a great Clerk, and reach the highest stature. Thus dost thou make proud knowledge bend and crouch.
 While Grace fills up uneven Nature.

 When creatures had no real light Inherent in them, thou didst make the sun,
Impute a lustre, and allow them bright:
 And in this show what Christ hath done.

That which before was darken'd clean
With bushy groves, pricking the looker's eye,
Vanish'd away, when Faith did change the scene:
And then appear'd a glorious sky.

 What though my body run to dust?
Faith cleaves unto it, counting every grain, With an exact and most particular trust,
 Reserving all for flesh again.

PRAYER.

Thayer, the Church's banquet, Angel's age,
 God's breath in man returning to his birth,
The soul in paraphrase, heart in pilgrimage,
 The Christian plummet sounding heaven and earth;'
 Engine against tit' Almighty, sinner's tower,
 Reversed thunder, Christ-side-piercing spear,
The six days' world-transposing in an hour,
 A kind of tune, which all things hear and fear;
 Softness, and peace, and joy, and love, and bliss,
Exalted Manna, gladness of the best,
Heaven in ordinary, men well drest, v
 Tho Milky Way, the bird of Paradise,
 Church-bells beyond tho stars heard, the soul's blood,
The land of spices, something understood.

HOLY COMMUNION.

 Not in rich furniture, or fine array,
Nor in a wedge of gold,
Thou, who from me wast sold,
To mo dost now thyself convey;
 For so thou should'st without me still have been, Leaving within me sin:
 But by the way of nourishment and strength,
 Thou crcop'st into my breast; Making thy way my rest,
And thy small quantities my length;
Which spread their forces into every part,
 Meeting sin's force and art.

 Yet can these not get over to my soul,
 Leaping the wall that parts Our souls

and fleshly hearts;
But as th' outworks, they may control
My rcbel-flesh, and, carrying thy name,
 Aflriyht both sin and shame.

Only thy grace, which with these elements comes,
 Knoweth the ready way, And hath the priy key,
Opening the soul's most subtile rooms:
Whilo those to spirits refined, at door attend
 Despatches from their friend.

 Give me my captive soul, or take
My body also thither.
 Another lift like this will make
 Them both to be together.

 Before that sin turn'd flesh to stone,
And all our lump to leaven;
 A fervent sigh might well have blown
Our innocent earth to heaven.

 For sure, when Adam did not know
To sin, or sin to smother;
lie might to heaven from Paradise go,
As from one room t' another.

 Thou hast restored us to this case
By this thy heavenly blood,
 Which I can go to, when I please,
 And leave th' earth to their food.

ANTiriloN.

Cho. Let all the world in every corner sing, *My God and King.*
Ver. The heavens arc not too high,
His praise may thither fly:
The earth is not too low,
His praises there may grow.
Cho. Let all the world in every corner sing, *My God and King.*
Ver. The Church with Psalms must shout,
 No door can keep them out:
But above all, the heart
Must bear the longest part.
Cho. Let all the world in every corner sing, *My God and King.*

 Immortal Love, author of this great frame,
 Sprung from that beauty which can never fade;
How hath man parcell'd out thy glorious name,
 And thrown it on that dust which thou hast made,
 While mortal love doth all the title gain!
Which siding with invention, they to-

gether
Bear all the sway, possessing heart and brain
(Thy workmanship), and give thec share in neither.

Wit fancies beauty, beauty raiscth wit:

The world is theirs; they two play out the game,
Thou standing by: and though thy glorious name
Wrought our deliverance from th' infernal pit,

Who sings thy praise? only a scarf or glove -/
Doth warm our hands, and make them write of love.

PART II.

IMMORTAL Heat, 0 let thy greater flame
Attract the lesser to it: let those fires
Which shall consume the world, first mako it tame,
And kindle in our hearts such true desires,

As may consume our lusts, and make thee way.

Then shall our hearts pant thee; then shall our brain All her inventions on thine Altar lay,
And there in hymns send back thy fire again:

D

Our eyes shall sec thee,-which before saw dust;
Dust blown by wit, till that they both wcro blind:
Thou shalt recover all thy goods in kind,
"Who wort disseized by usurping lust:

All knees shall bow to thee; all wits shall rise,
And praise Him who did make and mend our eyes.

TIIE TEMPER.

How should I praise thee, Lord! how should my rhymes
Gladly engrave thy love in steel,
If what my soul doth feel sometimes,
My soul might ever feel!

Although there were some forty heavens, or more,
Sometimes I peer above them all;
Sometimes I hardly reach a score,
Sometimes to hell I fall.

0 rack me not to such a vast extent;

Those distances belong to thee:
The world's too little for thy tent,
A grave too big for me.

Wilt thou meet arms with man, that thou dost stretch
A crumb of dust from heaven to hell?
Will great God measure with a wretch?
Shall ho thy stature spell?
0 let me, when thy roof my soul hath hid,
0 let me roost and nestle there:
Then of a sinner thou art rid,
And I of hope and fear.

Yet take thy way; for sure thy way is best:
Stretch or contract me thy poor debtor:
This is but tuning of my breast,
To make the music better.

Whether I fly with angels, fall with dust,
Thy hands made both, and I am there.
Thy power and love, my love and trust,
Make one place every where.

THE TEMPER.

It cannot bo. Where is that mighty joy, Which just now took up all my heart / Lord! if thou must needs use thy dart,

Save that, and me; or sin for both destroy.

The grosser world stands to thy word and art;
But thy diviner world of grace
Thou suddenly dost raise and raze,
And every day a new Creator art.
0 fix thy chair of grace, that all my powers
May also fix their reverence:
For when thou dost depart from hence,
They grow unruly, and sit in thy bowers.

Scatter, or bind them all to bcnd to thee:
Though elements change, and heaven move;
Let not thy higher Court remove,
But keep a standing Majesty in me.

JORDAN.

Who says that fictions only and false hair TV

Become a verse? Is there in truth no beauty?
Is all good structure in a winding stair /
May no lines pass, except they do their duty

Not to a true, but painted chair?
Is it not verse, except enchanted groves
And sudden arbours shadow coarse-spun lines 1
Must purling streams refresh a lover's loves?
Must all be veil'd, while he that reads, divines,
Catching the sense at two removes /

Shepherds arc honest people; let them sing:
Riddle who list, for me, and pidl for Prime:
I envy no man's nightingale or spring;
Nor let them punish me with loss of rhyme,
Who plainly say, *My God, my King.*

V EMPLOYMENT.

If as a flower doth spread and die,
Thou wouldst extend me to some good,
Before I were by frost's extremity
Nipt in the bud;

Which in thy garland I should fill, were mine
At thy great dooimx »&-;
For as thou dost impart thy grace,
The greater shall our glory be.
The measure of our joys is in this place,
The stuff with thee.

Let me not languish then, and spend
A life as barren to thy praise
As is the dust, to which that life doth tend,
But with delays.

All things arc busy: only I
Neither bring honey with the bees,
Nor flowers to make that, nor the husbandry
To water these.

I am no link of thy great chain,
But all my company is a weed.
Lord, place me in thy consort; give one strain t
To my pooru-eed,, 0 THE HOLY SCRIPTURES.

TART I. 0 Book! infinite sweetness! let my heart
Suck every letter, and a honey gain,
Precious for any grief in any part;
To clear the breast, to mollify all pain.

Thou art all health, health thriving, till it make
A full eternity: thou art a mass
Of strange delights, where we may

wish and take. Ladies, look here; this is
the thankful glass,

That mends the looker's eyes: this is
the well

That washes what it shows. Who can
endear

Thy praiso too much? thou art Heav-
en's Licgcr here,

Working against the states of death
and hell.

Thou art joy's handsel: heaven lies
flat in thee,

Subject to every mounter's bended
knee.

PART II.

Oh that I knew how all thy lights
combine,

And the configurations of their glory I

Seeing not only how each verse doth
shine,

But all the constellations of the story.

This verso marks that, and both do
make a motion

Unto a third, that ten leaves off doth lie:

Then as dispersed herbs do watch a potion,

These three make up some Christian's destiny.

Such arc thy secrets, which my life
makes good,

And comments on thee: for in every
thing

Thy words do find mo out, and parallels
bring,

And in another make me understood.

Stars are poor books, and oftentimes
do miss:

This book of stars lights to eternal bliss.

WHITSUNDAY.

Listen, sweet Dove, unto my song,

And spread thy golden wings in me;

Hatching my tender heart so long,

Till it get wing, and fly away with thee.

Where is that fire which once descended

On thy Apostles / thou didst then

Keep open house, richly attended,

Feasting all comers by twelve chosen
men.

Such glorious gifts thou didst bestow,

That th' earth did like a heaven appear:

The stars were coming down to know

If they might mend their wages, and
serve here.

The Sun, which once did shine alone,

Hung down his head, and wish'd for

night,

When he beheld twelve Suns for one

Going about the world, and giving light.

But since those pipes of gold, which
brought

That cordial water to our ground,

Were cut and martyr'd by the fault

Of those who did themselves through
their side wound;

Thou shutt'st the door, and kecp'st
within;

Scarce a good joy creeps through the
chink:

And if the braves of conquering sin

Did not excite thee, we should wholly
sink.

Lord, though we change, thou art the
same;

The same sweet God of love and light:

Restore this day, for thy great Name,

Unto his ancient and miraculous right.

GRACE.

My stock lies dead, and no increase

Doth my dull husbandry improve:

0 let thy graces without cease

Drop from above!

If still the Sun should hide his face,

Thy house would but a dungeon prove,

Thy works night's captives: 0 let grace

Drop from above!

The dew doth every morning fall;

And shall the dew outstrip thy Dove /

The dew, for which grass cannot call,

Drop from above.

Death is still working like a mole,

And digs my grave at each remove:

Let grace work too, and on my soul

Drop from above.

i

Sin is still hammering my heart

Unto a hardness, void of love:

Let suppling grace, to cross his art,

Drop from above.

0 come! for thou dost know the way.

Or if to me thou wilt not move,

Remove me where I need not say—

Drop from above.

PRAISE.

To write a verse or two, is all the praise

That I can raise:

Mend ray estate in any ways,

Thou shalt have more.

I go to Church; help me to wing., and
I

Will thither fly;

Or, if I mount unto the sky,

I will do more.

Man is all weakness; there is no such
thing

As Prince or King:

His arm is short; yet with a sling

He may do more.

An herb distill'd, and drunk, may
dwell next door,

Oa the same floor,

To a brave soul: Exalt the poor,

They can do more.

0 raise me, then! poor bees, that work
all day,

Sting my delay,

Avho have a work, as well as thcy,

And much, much more.

AFFLICTION.

Kill me not every day,

Thou Lord of life; since thy one death
for me

Is more than all my deaths can be,

Though I in broken pay

Die over each hour of Mcthusalem's
stay.

If all men's tears were let

Into one common sewer, sea, and brine;

What were they all, compared to thine?

Avhcrcin if they were set,

They would discolour thy most bloody
sweat.

Thou art my grief alone,

Thou Lord conceal it not: and as thoU
art

All my delight, so all my smart:

Thy cross took up in one,

By way of imprest all my future moan.,

MATINS. I Cannot ope mine eyes,

But thou art ready there to catch

My morning-soul and sacrifice:

Then wo must needs for that day inako
a match.

My God, what is a heart 1

Silver, or gold, or precious stone,

Or star, or rainbow, or a part

Of all these things, or all of them in one
1

My God, what is a heart, That thou
shouldst it so eye, and woo, Pouring upon it all thy art, As if that thou hadst
nothing else to do /

Indeed, man's whole estate Amounts
(and richly) to serve thee: He did not
heaven and earth create, Yet studies
them, not Him by whom they be.

Teach me thy love to know; That this
new light, which now I see, May both
the work, and workman show: Then by
a Sunbeam I will climb to thee.

SIN. 0 That I could a sin once see!
AVe paint the devil foul, yet he
Hath some good in him, all agree.
Sin is flat opposite to th' Almighty, see-
ing
It wants the good of *virtue,* and of *be-
ing.*
But God more care of us hath had,
    If apparitions make us sad,
    By sight of sin we should grow mad.
    Yet as in sleep we sco foul death, and
live;
    So devils arc our sins in prospective.

EVEN-SONG. Blest be the God of love,
Who gave me eyes, and light,.and pow-
er this day,
Both to be busy and to play.
But much more blest be God above,
Who gave me sight alone,
Which to himself ho did deny:
For when he sees my ways, I die:
But I have got his Son, and he hath
nono.
What have I brought thee home
For this thy love have I discharged the
debt,
"Which this day's favour did beget *I*
I ran; but all I brought, was foam.
Thy diet, care, and cost
Do end in bubbles, balls of wind;
Of wind to thee whom I have crost,
But balls of wild-fire to my troubled
mind.
Yet still thou goest on,
And now with darkness closest weary
eyes,
Saying to man, *It doth suffice:*
Henceforth repose; your work is done.
Thus in thy Ebony box
Thou dost enclose us, till the day
Put our amendment in our way,
And give new wheels to our disordcr'd
clocks.
I muse, which shows more love,
The day or night: that is the gale, this th'
harbour;
That is the walk, and this the arbour;
Or that the gardeu, this the grove.
My God, thou art all love.
Not one poor minute 'scapes thy breast,
But brings a favour from above;

And iu this love, more than in bed, I
rest.

CHURCH MONUMENTS.
While that my soul repairs to her devo-
tion,
Here I entomb my flesh, that it betimes
May take acquaintance of this heap of
dust;
To which the blast of death's incessant
motion,
Fed with the exhalation of our crimes,
Drives all at last. Therefore I gladly
trust
    My body to this school, that it may
learn
To spell his elements, and find his birth
Written in dusty heraldry and lines;
Which dissolution sure doth best dis-
cern,
Comparing dust with dust, and earth
with earth.
These laugh at Jet, and Marble put' for
signs,
    To sever the good fellowship of dust,
And spoil the meeting. What shall point
out them,
When they shall bow, and kneel, and
fall down flat
To kiss those heaps, which now they
have in trust?
Dear flesh, while I do pray, learn here
thy stem
And true descent; that when thou shalt
grow fat,
    And wanton in thy cravings, thou
may'st know,
That flesh is but the glass, which holds
the dust
That measures all our time; which also
shall
Be crumbled into dust. Mark here below,
How tame these ashes are, how free
from lust,
That thou may'st fit thyself against thy
fall.

CHURCH MUSIC.
    Sweetest of sweets, I thank you:
when displeasure Did through my body
wound my mind,
    You took me thence; and in your
house of pleasure A dainty lodging me
assign'd.
    Now I in you without a body moTC,
    Rising and falling with your wings:

"Wc both together sweetly live and
love,
    Yet say sometimes, *God help poor
Icings.*
    Comfort, 111 die; for if you post
from me,
Sure I shall do so, and much more:
    But if I travel in your company,
    You know the way to heaven's door.

CHURCH LOCK AND KEY.
I Know it is my sin, which locks thine
cars,
    And binds thy hands! Out-crying my
requests, drowning my tears; Or else the
chillness of my faint demands.
    But as cold hands arc angry with the
fire, And mend it still;
So I do lay the want of my desire,
Not on my sins, or coldness, but thy
will.
    Yet hear, 0 God, only for His blood's
sake,
    Which pleads for me: For though sins
plead too, yet like stones they make His
blood's sweet current much more loud
to be.

THE CHURCH FLOOR.
Mark you the floor? that square and
speckled stone,
Which looks so firm and strong,
Is *Patience:*
    And th' other black and grave,
wherewith each one
Is chequcr'd all along,
Humility:
    The gentle rising, which on cither
hand
Leads to the quire above,
Is *Confidence:*
    But the sweet cement, which in one
sure band
Ties the whole frame, is *Love*
And *Charity.*
    Hither sometimes Sin steals, and
stains The Marble's neat and curious
veins: But all is cleansed when the Mar-
ble weeps.
Sometimes Death, puffing at the door,
Blows all tho dust about the floor:
But while he thinks to spoil tho room,
he sweeps.
Blest be the *Architect,* whose art
Could build so strong in a weak heart.

TUB WINDOWS.
    Lord, how can man preach thy eternal

word?

He is a brittle crazy glass:

Yet in thy Temple thou dost him afford

This glorious and transcendent place,
To be a window, through thy grace.

But when thou dost anneal in glass
thy story,
Slaking thy life to shine within

The holy Preachers, then the light and
glory

More reverend grows, and more doth
win;
Which else shows watcrish, bleak, and
thin.

Doctrine and life, colours and light,
in one
"When they combine and mingle,
bring

A strong regard and awe: but speech
alone
Doth vanish like a flaring thing,
And in the car, not conscience ring.

TRINITY SUNDAY.

Lord, M'ho hast form'd me out of
mud,
And hast redeem'd me through thy
blood,
And sanctified inc to do good;

Purge all my sins done heretofore;
For I confess my heavy score,
And I will strive to sin no more.

Enrich my heart, mouth, hands in me,
With faith, with hope, with charity;
That I may run, rise, rest with thee.

CONTENT.

Peace, muttering thoughts, and do not
grudge to keep

Within the walls of your own breast.
Who cannot on his own bod sweetly
sleep,

Can on another's hardly rest.

Gad not abroad at every quest and
call Of an untrained hope or passion.
To court cach place or fortune that doth
fall,

Is wantonness in contemplation.

,JkIark how the fire in flints doth quiet
lie,

Content and warm to itself alone: But
when it would appear to other's eye,
Without a knock it never shone.

Give me the pliant mind, whose gentle measure

Complies and suits with all estates;

Which can let loose to a crown, and yet
with pleasure

Take up within a cloister's gates.

This soul doth span the world, and
hang content From cither pole unto the
centre:

Where in each room of the well-furnish'd tent

He lies warm, and without adventure.
E
The brags of life arc but a nine days'
wonder:
And after death tho fumes that spring

From private bodies, make as big a
thunder
As those which rise from a huge lving.

Only thy Chronicle is lost: and yet

Better by worms be all once spent,
Than to have hellish moths still gnaw
and fret Thy name in books, which may
not vent.

. When all thy deeds, whose brunt thou
fecl'st alone, Arc chaw'd by others'
pens and tongue, And as their wit is,
their digestion,

Thy nourish'd fame is weak or
strong.

Then cease discoursing, soul, till
thine own ground;

Do not thyself or friends importune.
IIo that by seeking hath himself once
found,

Hath ever found a happy fortune.

THE QUIDDITY.

Mv God, a verse is not a crown;
No poiut of honour, or gay suit,
No hawk, or banquet, or renown,
Nor a good sword, nor yet a lute:

It cannot vault, or dance, or play;
It never was in France or Spain;
Nor can it entertain the day
With a great stable or domain.

It is no office, art, or news;
Nor the Exchange, or busy Hall:
But it is that, which while I use,,
I am with thee, aud *Most take all.*

HUMILITY.

I Saw the Virtues sitting hand in hand

In several ranks upon an azure
throne,

Where all the beasts and fowls, by
their command,

Presented tokens of submission.

Humility, who sat the lowest there To
execute their call,

When by the beasts the presents tendcr'd were,

Gave them about to all.

The angry Lion did present his paw,
Which by consent was given to Mansuctude.

The fearful Hare her ears, which by
their law

Humility did reach to Fortitude.

The jealous Turkey brought his coral
chain,

That went to Temperance.

On Justice was bestow'd the Fox's
brain,

Kill'd in the way by chance.

At length the Crow, bringing the Peacock's plume

(For he would not), as they beheld the
grace

Of that brave gift, each one began to
fume,

And challenge it, as proper to his place,
Till they fell out; which when the beasts
espied,

They leapt upon the throne; And if
the Fox had lived to nile their side,

They had deposed each one.

Humility, who held tho plume, at this
Did weep so fast, that tho tears trickling
down
Spoil'd all the train: then saying, *Here it
is,*

For which ye wrangle, made them turn
their frown

Against tho beasts: so jointly bandying,
They drive them soon away;

And then amerced them, double gifts to
bring

At the next Session-day.

FRAILTY.

Lord, in my silence how do I despise
What upon trust
Is styled *honour, riches,* or *fair eyes;*
But is—-*fair dust!*
I surname them *gilded clay,*
Dear earth, fine grass, or *hay;*
In all, I think my foot doth ever tread
Upon their head.

But when I view abroad both Regiments,

The world's, and thine; Thine clad
with simpleness, and sad events; The
other fine, Full of glory and gay weeds,
Brave language, braver deeds: That
which was dust before, doth quickly

rise, And prick mine eyes.
0 brook not this, lest if what even now
My foot did tread,
    Affront those joys, wherewith thou didst endow,
And long since wed
My poor soul, e'en sick of love;
It may a Babel prove,
Commodious to couqucr heaven and thee
Planted in me.

CONSTANCY.

Who is the honest man?
He that doth still and strongly good pursue,
To God, his neighbour, and himself most true:
Whom neither force nor fawning can
Unpin, or wrench from giving all their due.
Whose honesty is not
So loose or easy, that a ruffling wind
Can blow away, or glittering look it blind:
Who rides his sure and even trot,
While the world now rides by, now lags behind.
Who, when great trials come,
Nor seeks, nor shuns them; but doth calmly stay,
Till he the thing and the example weigh:
All being brought into a sum,
What place or person calls for, he doth pay.
Whom none can work or woo,
To use in any thing a trick or sleight;
For above all things he abhors deceit:
His words and works and fashion too
All of a piece, and all are clear and straight.
Who never melts or thaws
At close temptations: when the day is done,
His goodness sets not, but in dark can run;
The sun to others writeth laws,
And is their virtue; Virtue is his Sun.
Who, when ho is to treat
With sick folks, women, those whom passions sway,
Allows for that, and keeps his constant way:
Whom others' faults do not defeat;
But though men fail him, yet his part doth play.

Whom nothing can procure,
When the wide world runs bias, from his will   .
To writhe his limbs, and share, not mend the ill.
This is the Marksman, safe and sure,
Who still is right, and prays to be so still.

AFFLICTION.

My heart did heave, and there came forth, *0 God!*
By that I knew that thou wast in the grief,
To guide and govern it to my relief,
Making a sceptre of the rod:
Hadst thou not had thy part,
Sure the unruly sigh had broke my heart.
    But since thy breath gave mo both life and shape,
Thou know'st my tallies; and when there's assign'd
So much breath to a sigh, what's then behind *l*
Or if some years with it escape,
The sigh then only is
A gale to bring me sooner to my bliss.
    Thy life on earth was grief, and thou art still
    Constant unto it, making it to be
    A point of honour, now to grieve in me,
    And in thy members suffcr ill. They who lament one cross, Thou dying daily, praise thee to thy loss.

THE STAR.

Brtojit spark, shot from a brighter place,
Where beams surround my Saviour's face,
Canst thou be any where
So well as there?
    Yet, if thou wilt from thence depart,
Take a bad lodging in my heart;
For thou canst make a debtor,
And make it better.
    First with thy fire-work burn to dust
Folly, and worse than folly, lust:
Then with thy light refine,
And make it shine.
    So disengaged from sin and sickness,
Touch it with thy celestial quickness,
That it may hang and move
After thy love.
    Then with our trinity of light,
    Motion, and heat, let's take our flight

Unto the place where thou
Before didst bow.
    Get me a standing there, and place
    Among the beams, which crown the face
Of Him who died to part
Sin and my heart:
    That so among the rest I may
    Glitter, and curl, and wind as they:
That winding is their fashion
Of adoration.
    Sure thou wilt joy, by gaining me
To fly home like a laden bee
Unto that hive of beams
And garland-streams.

SUNDAY.

0 Day most calm, most bright, The fruit of this, the next world's bud, Th' indorsement of supreme delight, Writ by a friend, and with his blood; The couch of time; care's balm and bay; The week were dark, but for thy light:
    Thy Torch doth show the way.
    The other days and thou Make up one man; whose face thou art, Knocking at heaven with thy brow: Tho workingdays are the back-part; The burden of the week lies there, Making the whole to stoop and bow,
    Till thy release appear.
Man had straight forward gone
To endless death; but thou dost pull
And turn us round to look on one,
Whom, if we were not very dull,
We could not choose but look on still;
Since there is no place so alone
The which he doth not fill.
Sundays the pillars are,
On which heaven's palace arched lies:
The other days fill up the spare
And hollow room with vanities.
They are the fruitful beds and borders
In God's rich garden: that is bare
Which parts their ranks and orders.
The Sundays of man's life,
Threaded together on time's string,
Make bracelets to adorn the wife
Of the eternal glorious King.
On Sunday heaven's gate stands ope;
Blessings are plentiful and rife,
More plentiful than hope.
This day my Saviour rose,
And did enclose this light for his:
That, as each beast his manger knows,
Man might not of his fodder miss.

Christ hath took in this piece of ground,
And made a garden there for those
Who want herbs for their wound.

The Rest of our Creation Our great
Redeemer did remove

With the same shake, which at his
passion
Did th' earth and all things with it move.
As Samson bore the doors away,
Christ's hands, though nail'd, wrought
our salvation,
And did unhinge that day.
The brightness of that day
"We sullied by our foul offence:
Wherefore that robe we cast away,
Having a new at his expense,
Whose drops of blood paid the full
price,
That was required to make us gay,
    And fit for Paradise.
Thou art a day of mirth:
And where the week-days trail on
ground,
Thy flight is higher, as thy birth:
0 let mo take thee at the bound,
Leaping with thee from seven to seven,
Till that we both, being toss'd from
earth,
Fly hand in hand to heaven!

AVARICE.

Monet, thou banc of bliss, and source of
woe,
    Whence comest thou, that thou art so
fresh and fine? I know thy parentage is
base and low:
    Man found thee poor and dirty in a
mine.
    Surely thou didst so little contribute
    To this great kingdom, which thou
now hast got,
That he was fain, when thou wast destitute,
    To dig thee out of thy dark cave and
grot.
    Then forcing thee, by fire he made
thcc bright: " Nay, thou hast got the face
of man; for we
    Have with our stamp and seal trans-
fcrr'd our right; Thou art the man, and
man but dross to thee.
    Man calleth thee his wealth, who
made thee rich; And while he digs out
thee, falls in the ditch.
    How well her name an *Army* doth
present,

In whom the *Lord of hods* did pitch his
tent!

TO ALL ANGELS AND SAINTS.

0 Glorious spirits, who after all your
bands
See the smooth face of God, without a
frown,
Or strict commands;
Where every one is king, and hath his
crown,
If not upon his head, yet in his hands:
Not out of envy or maliciousness
Do I forbear to crave your special aid.
I would address
My vows to thee most gladly, blessed
Maid,
And Mother of my God, in my distress:
    Thou art the holy mine, whence came
the gold,
The great restorative for all decay
In young and old;
Thou art the cabinet where the jewel
lay:
Chiefly to thee would I my soul unfold.
    But now, alas! I dare not; for our
King,
Whom we do all jointly adore and
praise,
Bids no such thing:
And where his pleasure no injunction
lays
('Tis your own case), ye never move a
wing.
    All worship is prerogative, and a
flower
Of his rich crown, from whom lies no
appeal
At the last hour:
Therefore wo dare not from his garland
steal,
To make a posic for inferior power.
    Although then others court you, if ye
know
What's done on earth, we shall not fare
the worse
Who do not so;
Since we are ever ready to disburse,
If any one our Master's hand can show.

EMPLOYMENT.

    He that is weary, let him sit.
My soul would stir '
And trade in courtesies and wit,
Quitting the fur,
To cold complexions needing it.
Man is no star, but a quick coal

Of mortal fire:
    Who blows it not, nor doth control
A faint desire,
    Lets his own ashes choke his soul.
    When th' elements did for place con-
test
With Him, whose will
    Ordain'd the highest to be best:
The earth sat still,
    And by the others is opprest.
    Life is a business, not good cheer;
Ever in wars.
The sun still shineth there or here,
Whereas the stars
Watch an advantage to appear.
0 that I were an Orange-trcc, That busy
plant!
Then I should ever laden be,
And never want
Some fruit for him that dresscth me.
    But we are still too young or old; The
man is gone,
Before we do our wares unfold:
So we freeze on,
Until the grave increase our cold.

DENIAL.

    When my devotions could not pierce
Thy silent ears; Then was my heart broken, as was my verse; My breast was
full of fears
    And disorder,
    My bent thoughts, like a brittle bow,
    Did fly asunder: Each took his way;
some would to pleasures go, Some to
the wars and thunder Of alarms.
    As good go any where, they say,
    As to benumb Both knees and heart,
in crying night and day, *Come, come,
my God, 0 come,*
    But no hearing.
0 Thou that shouldst give dust a tongue
To cry to thee, And then not hear it crying! all day long My heart was in my
knee,
    But no hearing.
    Therefore my soul lay out of sight,
Untuned, unstrung:
My feeble spirit, unable to look right,
Like a nipt blossom, hung
    Discontented.
0 cheer and tunc my heartless breast,
Defer no time; That so thy favours
granting my request, They aud my mind
may chime,
    And mend my rhyme.

CHRISTMAS.

All after pleasures as I rid one day,
My horse and I, both tired, body and mind,
With full cry of affections, quite astray;
I took up in the next Inn I could find.
There when I came, whom found I but my dear,
My dearest Lord, expecting till the grief
Of pleasures brought me to him, ready there
To be all passengers' most sweet relief?
O Thou, whose glorious, yet contracted light, Wrapt in night's mantle, stole into a manger; Since my dark soul and brutish is thy right,
To Man of all beasts bo not thou a stranger:
Furnish and deck my soul, that thou may'st have
A better lodging, than a rack, or grave.

The shepherds sing; and shall I silent be *l*
My God, no hymn for thee?
My soul's a shepherd too: a Hock it feeds
Of thoughts, and words, and deeds.
The pasture is thy word; the streams, thy grace Enriching all the place.
Shepherd and flock shall sing, and all my powers
Out-sing the daylight hours.
Then we will chide the Sun for letting night
Take up his place and right:
We sing one common Lord; wherefore he should
Himself the candle hold
I will go searching, till I find a Sun
Shall stay, till wo have done;
A willing shiner, that shall shine as gladly,
As frost-nipt Suns look sadly.
Then we will sing, and shine all our own day,
And one another pay:
His beams shall cheer my breast, and both so twine,
Till even his beams sing, and my music shine.

UNGRATEFULNESS.

Loud, with what bounty and rare clemency
Hast thou redcem'd us from the grave!

If thou hadst let us run,
Gladly had man adored the Sun,
And thought his god most brave;
Where now we shall be better gods than he.
Thou hast but two rare Cabinets full of treasure,
The *Trinity,* and *Incarnation:*
Thou hast unlock'd them both,
And made them jewels to betroth
The work of thy creation
Unto thyself in everlasting pleasure.
The statelier Cabinet is the *Trinity,*
Whose sparkling light access denies:
Therefore thou dost not show
This fully to us, till death blow
The dust into our eyes;
For by that powder thou wilt make us see.
But all thy sweets arc pack'd up in the other; Thy mercies thither flock and flow; That, as the first affrights,
This may allure us with delights;
Because this box we know;
For wc have all of us just such another.
But man is close, reserved, and dark to thee;
When thou demandest but a heart,
He cavils instantly.
In his poor cabinet of bone
Sins have thcir box apart,
Defrauding thee, who gavest two for one.

SIGHS AND GROANS.

O no not use me
After my sins! look not on my desert,
But on thy glory! then thou wilt reform,
And not refuse me: for thou only art
The mighty God, but I a silly worm:
O do not bruise me! O do not urge mc!
For what account can thy ill steward make *l* I have abused thy stock, destroy'd thy woods, Suck'd all thy magazines: my head did ache, Till it found out how to consume thy goods: O do not scourge me! O do not blind me! I have deserved that an Egyptian night Should thicken all my powers; because my lust p
Hath still scw'd fig-leaves to exclude thy light: But I ain frailty, and already dust: O do not grind me!
O do not fill mo
With the turn'd vial of thy bitter wrath!
For thou hast other vessels full of blood,

A part whereof my Saviour emptied hath,
Eveu uuto death: since he died for my good,
O do not kill me!
But O, reprieve me I For thou hast *life* and *death* at thy command; Thou art both *Judge* and *Saviour, feast* and *rod, Cordial* and *Corrosive:* put not thy hand
Into the bitter box; but, O my God,
My God, relieve me!

THE WORLD.

Love built a stately house; where *Fortune* came
And spinning fancies, she was heard to say,
That her fine cobwebs did support the frame,
Whereas they were supported *by* tho same:
But *Wisdom* quickly swept them all away.
Then *Pleasure* came, who, liking not the fashion,
Began to make *Balconies, Terraces,*
Till she had wcakcu'd all by alteration:
But reverend *laius,* and many a *proclamation*
Reformed all at length with menaces.
Then entcr'd *Sin,* and with that Sycamore,
"Whose leaves first shcltcr'd man from drought and dew,
"Working and winding slily evermore,
The inward walls and summers cleft and tore:
But *Grace* shored these, and cut that as it grew.
Then *Sin* combincd with *Death* in a firm band,
To raze the building to the very floor:
Which they effected, none could them withstand;
But *Love* and *Grace* took *Glory* by the hand,
And built a braver palace than before.

COLOSSIANS III. 3.

" OUK LIFE IS HID WITH CHKIST IN COD." *My* words and thoughts do both express this notion,
That *Life* hath with the sun a double motion.
The first *Is* straight, and our diurnal friend;

The other *Hid,* and doth obliquely bend.
One life is wrapt *In* flesh, and tends to earth:
The otherwinds toward *Him,* whose happy birth
Taught me to live here so, *That* still one eye
Should aim and shoot at that which *Is* on high;
Quitting with daily labour all *My* pleasure,
To gain at harvest an eternal *Treasure.*

VANITY.

The fleet Astronomer can bore And thread the spheres with his quick-piercing mind: lie views their stations, walks from door to door, Surveys, as if he had design'd
To make a purchase there: he sees their dances
And knoweth long before,
Both their full-eyed aspects, and secret glances.
The nimble Diver with his side
Cuts through the working waves, that he may fetch
Ilia dearly-earned pearl, which God did hide
On purpose from the venturous wretch;
That he might save his life, and also hers,
Who with excessive pride
Her own destruction and his danger wears.
The subtle Chymic can divest
And strip the creature naked, till he find
The callow principles within their nest:
There he imparts to them his mind,
Admitted to their bed-chamber, before
They appear trim and drest To ordinary suitors at the door.
What hath not man sought out and found, But his dear God 1 who yet his glorious law Embosoms in us, mellowing the ground
" With showers and frosts, with love and awe; So that we need not say, Where's this command 1
Poor man! thou scarchest round To find out *death,* but missest *life* at hand.

LENT.

Welcome, dear feast of Lent: who loves not thee, He loves not Temperance, or Authority,
But is composed of passion. The Scriptures bid *uafasl;* the Church says, Now: Givo to thy Mother what thou wouldst allow
To every Corporation.
The humble soul, composed of lovo and fear,
Begins at home, and lays the burden there,
When doctrines disagree:
He says, In things which use hath justly got,
I am a scandal to the Church, and not
The Church is so to me.
True Christians should be glad of an occasion
To use their temperance, seeking no evasion,
When good is seasonable;
Unless Authority, which should increase
The obligation in us, make it less,
And Power itself disable.
Besides the cleanness of sweet abstinence,
Quick thoughts and motions at a small expense,
A face not fearing light:
Whereas in fulness there arc sluttish fumes,
Sour exhalations, and dishonest rheums,
Revenging the delight.
Then those same pendent profits, which the spring
And Easter intimate, enlarge the thing,
And goodness of the deed.
Neither ought other men's abuse of Lent
Spoil the good use; lest by that argument
We forfeit all our Creed.
Tis true, wo cannot rcach Christ's fortieth day;
Yet to go part of that religious way
Is better than to rest:
We cannot reach our Saviour's purity;
Yet arc we bid, *Be holy even as he.*
In both let's do our best.
Who gocth in the way which Christ hath gone. Is much more sure to meet with him, than one
That travelleth by-ways. Perhaps my God, though he be far before, May turn, and take me by the hand, and more,
May strengthen my decays.
Yet, Lord, instruct us to improve our fast
By starving sin, and taking such repast
As may our faults control:
That every man may revel at his door,
Not in his parlour; banqueting the poor,
And among those his soul.

VIRTUE.

Sweet Day, so cool, so calm, so bright,
The bridal of the earth and sky,
The dew shall weep thy fall to-night;
For thou must die.
Sweet Rose, whose hue angry and brave
Bids the rash gazer wipe his eye,
Thy root is ever in its grave,
And thou must die.
Sweet Spring, full of sweet days and roses,
A box where sweets compacted lie,
My Music shows ye have your closes,
And all must die.
Only a sweet and virtuous soul,
Like scason'd timber, never gives;
But though the whole world turn to coal,
Then chiefly lives.

THE PEARL.

MATT. XIII.

I Know the ways of Learning; both the head
And Pipes that feed the press, and make it run;
What Reason hath from Nature borrowed,
Or of itself, like a good housewife, spun
In laws and policy; what the stars conspire,
What willing Nature speaks, what forced by fire;
Both tli' old discoveries, and the new-found seas,
The stock and surplus, cause and history:
All these stand open, or I have the keys:
Yet I love thee.

i

I know the ways of Honour, what maintains
The quick returns of courtesy and wit:
In vies of favours whether party gains,
When glory swells the heart, and mouldeth it
To all expressions both of hand and eye,
Which on the world a true-love-knot

may tie,
And bear the bundle, whcresoc'cr it
goes:
How many drams of spirit there must bo
To sell my life unto my friends or foes:
Yet I love thee.

I know the ways of Pleasure, the
sweet strains,
The lullings and the relishes of it;
The propositions of hot blood and
brains;
What mirth and music mean; what love
and wit
Have done these twenty hundred years,
and moro:
I know the projects of unbridled store:
My stufF is flesh, not brass; my senses
live,
And grumble oft, that they have more in
mo
Than he that curbs them, being but ono
to five:
Yet I love thee.

I know all these, and have them in my
hand:
Therefore not scaled, but with open
eyes
I fly to thee, and fully understand
Both the main sale, and the commodi-
ties;
And at what rate and price I have thy
love;
With all tho circumstances that may
move:
Yet through the labyrinths, not my
grovelling wit,
But thy silk-twist let down from heaven
to me,
Did both conduct and teach me, how by
it
To climb to thec.

AFFLICTION.

Broken in pieces all asunder,
Lord, hunt mo not,
A thing forgot,
Once a poor creature, now a wonder,
A wonder tortured in the space
Betwixt this world and that of grace.

My thoughts arc all a case of knives,
Wounding my heart
With scattcr'd smart;
As watering-pots give flowers their
lives.
Nothing their fury can control,
While they do wound and prick my

soul.
All ray attendants arc at strife,
Quitting their place
Unto my face:
Nothing performs the task of life:
The elements arc let loose to fight,
And while I live, try out their right.

Oh, help, my God! let not their plot
Kill them and me,
Ami also thee,
Who art my life: dissolve the knot,
As the sun scatters by his light
All the rebellions of the night.

o
Then shall those powers, which work
for grief,
Enter thy pay,
And day by day
Labour thy praise and my relief;
With care and courage building me,
Till I reach heaven, and much more,
thee.

MAN.

My God, I heard this day, That none
doth build a stately habitation But he
that means to dwell therein. What house
more stately hath there been, Or can be,
than is Man l to whose creation All
things are in decay.

For Man is every thing,
And more: He is a tree, yet bears no
fruit;
A beast, yct is, or should be more:
Reason and speech wc only bring.
Parrots may thank us, if they arc not
mute,
They go upon the score.
Man is all symmetry,
Full of proportions, one limb to another,
And all to all the world besides:
Each part may call the farthest, brother:
For head with foot hath private amity,
And both with moons and tides.

Nothing hath got so far, But Man
hath caught and kept it, as his prey. His
eyes dismount the highest star He is in
little all the sphere. Herbs gladly cure
our flesh, because that they Find their
acquaintance there.

For us the winds do blow; The earth
doth rest, heaven move, and fountains
flow. Nothing we see, but means our
good, As our *delight*, or as our *treasure:*
The whole is, cither our cupboard ol-
food, Or cabinet of *incisure.* The stars

have us to bed;
Night draws the curtain, which the Sun
withdraws:
Music and light attend our head.
All things unto *over flesh* are kind
In their *descent* and *being;* to our *mind*
In their *ascent* and *cause.*
Each thing is full of duty:
Waters united, are our navigation;
Distinguished, our habitation;
Below, our drink; above, our meat:
Both arc our cleanliness. I lath one such
beauty?
Then how arc all things neat!
o More servants wait on Man,
Than he'll take notice of: in every path
He treads down that which doth be-
friend him,
When sickness makes him pale and
wan.
Oh, mighty love! Man is one world, and
hath
Another to attend him.
Since then, my God, thou hast
So brave a Palace built; 0 dwell in it,
That it may dwell with thee at last!
Till then, afford us so much wit,
That, as the world serves ifs, wc may
serve thee,
And both thy servants be.
' Distinguished,' *i. e.,* when marked by
au island.

ANT1PII0N.

Chor. Praised bo the God of love,
Men. Here below,
Angels. And here above:
Chor. Who hath dealt his mercies so,
And. To his friend,
Men. And to his foe;
Chor. That both grace and glory tend
Ano. Us of old,
Men. And us in the end.
Chor. The great Shepherd of the fold
Ano. Us did make,
Men. For us was sold.
Chor. He our foes in pieces brake:
Ano. Him we touch;
Men. And him we take.
Chor. Wherefore since that he is
such,
Ano. We adore,
Men. And we do crouch.
Chor. Lord, thy praises shall be more.
Men. Wc have none,
Ano. And we no store.

Chor. Praised be the God alone
Who hath made of two folds one. UN-
KINDNESS.

Lord, make me coy and tender to of-
fend:
In friendship, first I think, if that agree,
Which I intend,
Unto my friend's intent and end.
I would not use a friend, as I use Thee.

If any touch my friend, or his good
name,
It is my honour and my love to free
His blasted fame
From the least spot or thought of blame.
I could not use a friend, as I use Thee.

My friend may spit upon my curious
floor:
Would he have gold / I lend it instantly;
But lot the poor,
And thou within them, starve at door.
I cannot use a friend, as I use Thee.

When that my friend pretendcth to a
place,
I quit my interest, and leave it free:
But when thy grace
Sues for my heart, I thee displace;
Nor would I use a fricnd, as I use Thee.

Yet can a friend what Thou hast done
fulfil / 0 write in brass, *My God upon
a tree His blood did spill, Only to purchase my good-mil: Yet use I not my
foes, as I use Tliee.* LIFE.

I Made a posie, while the day ran by:
Here will I smell my remnant out, and
tic
My life within this band.
But time did beckon to the flowers, and
they
By noon most cunningly did steal away,
And withcr'd in my hand.

.My hand was next to them, and then
my heart; I took, without more thinking,
in good part
Time's gentle admonition; Who did
so sweetly death's sad taste convey,
Making my mind to smell my fatal day,
Yet sugaring the suspicion.

Farewell, dear flowers, sweetly your
time yo spent, Fit, while ye lived for
smell or ornament,
And after death for cures. I follow
straight without complaints or grief,
Since if my scent be good, I care not if
It bo as short as yours.
SUBMISSION.

But that thou art my wisdom, Lord,
And both mine eyes arc thine,
My mind would be extremely stirr'd
For missing my design.
Were it not better to bestow
Some place and power on me?
Then should thy praises-with mo
grow,
And share in my degree.

But when I thus dispute and grieve, I
do resume my sight;
And pilfering what I once did give,
Disseize thee of thy right.
How know I, if thou shouldst me
raise, That I should then raise thee?
Perhaps great places and thy praise
Do not so well agree.

Wherefore unto my gift I stand; I will
no more advise:
Only do thou lend me a hand,
Since thou hast both mine eyes.
JUSTICE.

I Cannot skill of these thy ways: *Lord,
thou didst make me, yet thou ivoundest
me. Lord, thou dost wound me, yet thou
dost relieve me: Lord, thou rclicvcst, yet
I die by thee: Lord, thou dost kill me, yet
thou dost reprieve me.*

But when I mark my life and praise,
Thy justice me most fitly pays:
For, i" *do praise thee, yet I praise thee
not:
My prayers mean thee, yet my prayers
stray:
I would do well, yet sin the hand hath
got:
My soul doth love thee, yet it loves de-
lay.*

I cannot skill of these my ways.
CHARMS AND KNOTS.

Who read a Chapter when they rise,
Shall ne'er be troubled with ill eyes.

A poor man's rod, when thou dost
ride,
Is both a weapon and a guide.

Who shuts his hand, hath lost his
gold:
Who opens it, hath it twice told.

Who goes to bed, and doth not pray,
Makcth two nights to every day.

Who by aspersions throw a stone
At the head of others, hit their own.

Who looks on ground with humble
eyes,
Finds himself there, and seeks to rise.

When the hair is sweet through pride
or lust,
The powder doth forget the dust.

Take one from ten, and what remains?
Ten still, if Sermons go for gains.

In shallow waters heaven doth show:
But who drinks on, to hell may go.
AFFLICTION.

My God, I read this day,
That planted Paradise was not so firm
As was and is thy floating Ark; whoso
stay
And anchor thou art only, to confirm
And strengthen it iu every age,
When waves do rise, and tempests rage.

At first wc lived in pleasure;
Thine own delights thou didst to us im-
part:
When wc grew wanton, thou didst use
displeasure
To make us thine: yet that we might not
part,
As wc at first did board with thee,
Now thou wouldst taste our misery.

There is but joy and grief;
If cither will convert us, we arc thine:
Some angels used the first; if our relief
Take up the second, then thy double line
And several baits in cither kind
Furnish thy table to thy mind.

Affliction then is ours; We are the
trees, whom shaking fastens more,
While blustering winds destroy the
wanton bowers, And ruffle all their curious knots and store. My God, so temper joy and woe, That thy bright beams
may tame thy bow.

MORTIFICATION. How soon doth man
decay!
When clothes arc taken from a chest of
sweets
To swaddle infants, whose young breath
Scarce knows the way;
Those clouts arc little winding-
sheets, Which do consign and send
them unto death.

When boys go first to bed,
They step into their voluntary graves;
Sleep binds them fast; only their breath
Makes them not dead.

Successive nights, like rolling waves,
Convey them quickly, who aro bound
for death.

When youth is frank.and free,

And calls for music, while his veins do swell,
All day exchanging mirth and breath
In company;
That music summons to the knell,
Which shall befriend him at the house of death.
When man grows staid and wise,
Getting a house and home, where ho may move
Within the circle of his breath,
Schooling his eyes;
That dumb enclosure makcth love
Unto the coinn, that attends his death.
When age grows low and weak,
Marking his grave, and thawing every year, Till all do melt, and drown his breath When he would speak;
A chair or litter shows the bier
Which shall convey him to the house of death.
Man, ere he is aware,
Hath put together a solemnity,
And dress'd his hearse, while he has breath
As yet to spare.
Yet, Lord, instruct us so to die,
That all these dyings may be life in death.

DECAY.

Sweet were the days, when thou didst lodge with *Lot,*
Struggle with *Jacob,* sit with *Gideon,*
Advise with *Abraham,* when thy power could not
Encounter *Moses* strong complaints and moan:
Thy words Mere then, *Let me alone.*
One might have sought and found thee presently
At some fair oak, or bush, or cave, or well:
Is my God this way? No, they would reply;
lie is to *Sinai* gone, as we heard tell:
List, ye may hear great *Aaron's* bell.
But now thou dost thyself immure and close
In some one corner of a feeble heart:
Where yet both Sin and Satan, thy old foes,
Do pinch and straiten thee, and use much art
To gain thy thirds and little part.
I see the world grows old, when as

the heat
Of thy great love once spread, as in an urn
Doth closet up itself, and still retreat,
Cold sin still forcing it, till it return,
And calling Justice, all things burn.

MISERY.

Lord, let the Angels praise thy name.
Man is a foolish thing, a foolish thing;
Folly and Sin play all his game. His house still burns; and yet he still doth sing, *Man is but grass, lie knows it, fill the glass.* How canst thou brook his foolishness *l*
Why, he'll not loso a cup of drink for thee:
Bid him but temper his excess;
Not he: he knows, where he can better be,
As he will swear,
Than to serve thee in fear.
What strange pollutions doth he wed,
And make his own? as if none knew, but he.
No man shall beat into his head That thou within his curtains drawn canst sec: They arc of cloth, Where never yet came moth.
Tho best of men, turn but thy hand
For one poor minute, stumble at a pin:
They would not have their actions scann'd,
Nor any sorrow tell them that they sin,
Though it bo small
And measure not their fall.
Thcy quarrel thco, and would give over The bargain made to servo thee: but thy love
Holds them unto it, and doth cover
Their follies with the wing of thy mild Dove,
Not suffering those
Who would, to be thy foes.
My God, Man cannot praise thy name:
Thou art all brightness, perfect purity;
The Sun holds down his head for shame, Dead with eclipses, when we speak of thee. How shall infection Presume on *thy* perfection *l* As dirty hands foul all they touch,
And those things most, which arc most pure and fine:
So our clay hearts, even when we crouch
To sing thy praises, make them less di-

vine.
Yet cither this
Or none thy portion is.
Man cannot serve thee; let him go
And serve the swine: there, there is his delight:
lie doth not like this virtue, no;
Give him his dirt to wallow in all night;
These Preachers make
His head to shoot and ache.
0 foolish man! where arc thine eyes?
How hast thou lost them in a crowd of cares?
Thou pull'st the rug, and wilt not rise,
No, not to purchase the whole pack of stars
There let them shine,
Thou must go sleep, or dine.
The bird that sees a dainty bower
Made in the tree, where she was wont to sit,
Wonders and sings, but not his power
"Who made the arbour: this exceeds her wit.
But Man doth know
The spring whence all things flow:
And yet, as though he knew it not,
His knowledge winks, and lets his humours reign:
They make his life a constant blot,
And all the blood of God to run in vain.
Ah, wretch! what verso
Can tlrv strange ways rehearse l
Indeed at first Man Mas a treasure,
A box of jewels, shop of rarities,
A ring, whose posic was, *My pleasure:*
lie was a garden in a Paradise:
Glory and grace
Did crown his heart and face.
But sin hath fool'd him. Now he is
A lump of flesh, without a foot or wing,
To raise him to the glimpse of bliss:
A sick toss'd vessel, dashing on each thing;
Nay, his own shelf:
My God, I mean myself.

JORDAN.

When first my lines of heavenly joys made mention,
Such was their lustre, they did so excel,
That I sought out quaint words, and trim invention; My thoughts began to burnish, sprout, and swell, Curling with metaphors a plain intention, Decking

the scuse, as if it were to sell.

Thousands of notions in my brain did run,

Offering their service, if I were not sped:

I often blotted what I had begun;

This was not quick enough, and that was dead.

Nothing could seem too rich to clothe the Sun,

Much less those joys which trample on his head.

As flames do work and wind, when they ascend;

So did I weave myself into the sense.

But while I bustled, I might hear a friend

Whisper, *How wide is all this long pretence!*

There is in love a sweetness ready penn'd:

Copy out only that, and save expense.

PRAYER.

Op what an easy quick access,

My blessed Lord, art thou! how suddenly

May our requests thine ear invade!

To show that state dislikes not easiness,

If I but lift mine eyes, my suit is made:

Thou canst no more not hear, than thou canst die.

Of what supreme Almighty power Is thy great arm which spans the East and West,

And tacks the Centre to'the Sphere!

By it do all things live their measured hour: We cannot ask the thing, which is not there, Blaming the shallowness of our request.

Of what immeasurable love

Art thou possest, who, when thou couldst not die,

Wert fain to take our flesh and curse,

And for our sakes in person sin reprove;

That by destroying that which tied thy purse,

Thou might'st make way for liberality!

Since then these three wait on thy throne, *Ease, Power,* and *Love;* I value Prayer so,

That were I to leave all but one, Wealth, fame, endowments, virtues, all should go; I and dear Prayer would together dwell, And quickly gain, for each inch lost, an ell.

OBEDIENCE. My God, if writings may

Convey a lordship any way

Whither the buyer and the seller please;

Let it not thee displease;

If this poor paper do as much as they..'

On it my heart doth bleed

As many lines, as there doth need

To pass itself and all it hath to thee.

To which I do agree,

And here present it as my special deed.

If that hereafter Pleasure

Cavil, and claim her part and measure,

As if this passed with a reservation,

Or some such words in fashion;

I here exclude the wrangler from thy treasure.

0 let thy sacred Mill All thy delight in me fulfil! Let me not think an action mine own way,

But as thy love shall sway, Resigning up the rudder to thy skill Lord, what is man to thee,

That thou shouldst mind a rotten tree?

Yet since thou canst not choose but sec my actions;

So great arc thy perfections,

Thou may'st as well my actions guide, as see.

Besides, thy death and blood

Show'd a strange love to all our good:

Thy sorrows were in earnest; no faint proffer,

Or superficial offer

Of what we might not take, or be withstood.

Wherefore I all forego:

To one word only I say, No:

Where in the deed there was an intimation

Of a *gift* or *donation,*

Lord, let it now by way of *purchase* go.

lie that will pass his land,

As I have mine, may set his hand

And heart unto this deed, when he hath read;

And make the purchase spread

To both our goods, if he to it will stand.

How happy were my part,

If some kind man would thrust his heart

Into these lines; till in Heaven's court of rolls

They were by winged souls

Entcr'd for both, far above their desert!

CONSCIENCE.

Peace, prattler, do not lour:

Not a fair look, but thou dost call it foul:

Not a sweet dish, but thou dost call it sour:

Music to thee doth howl.

By listening to thy chatting fears

I have both lost mine eyes and cars.

Prattler, no more, I say:

My thoughts must work, but like a noiseless sphere.

Harmonious peace must rock them all the day:

No room for prattlers there.

If thou pcrsistest, I will tell thee,

That I have physic to expel thee.

And the receipt shall be

My Saviour's blood: whenever at his board

I do but taste it, straight it cleanscth me,

And leaves thec not a word;

No, not a tooth or nail to scratch,

And at my actions carp, or catch.

Yet if thou talkest still,

Besides my physic, know there's some for thec:

Some wood and nails to make a staff or bill

For those that trouble me:

The bloody cross of my dear Lord

Is both my physic and my sword.

SION.

Lord, with what glory wast thou served of old,

When *Solomon's* temple stood and flourished!

Where most things were of purest gold;

The wood was all embellished

With flowers and carvings, mystical and rare:

All show'd the builder's, craved the seer's care.

Yet all this glory, all this pomp and state,

Did not affect thee much, was not thy aim;

Something there was that sow'd debate:

Wherefore thou quitt'st thy ancient claim:

And now thy Architecture meets with sin;

For all thy frame and fabric is within.

There thou art struggling with a peevish heart,

Which sometimes crosscth thee, thou

sometimes it
  The fight is hard on cither part.
  Great God doth fight, he doth submit.
  All *Solomon's* sea of brass and world
of stone
  Is not so dear to thee as one good
groan.
  And truly brass and stones arc heavy
things,
Tombs for the dead, not temples fit for
thee:
  But groans arc quick, and full of
wings,
And all their motions upward be;
  And ever as they mount, like larks
they sing:
  The note is sad, yet music for a king.
HOME.
Come, Lord, my head doth burn, my
heart is sick,
  While thou dost ever, ever stay:
  Thy long deferrings wound me to the
quick,
  My spirit gaspeth night and day.
0 show thyself to me,
  Or take me up to thee!
  How canst thou stay, considering the
pace
  The blood did make, which thou didst
waste?
  When I behold it trickling down thy
face,
I never saw thing make such haste.
0 show thyself, &c.
  When man was lost, thy pity look'd
about,
To see what help in th' earth or sky:
  But there was none; at least no help
without:
The help did in thy bosom lie.
0 show thyself, &e.
  There lay thy Son: and must ho leave
that nest,
That hive of sweetness, to rcmovo
  Thraldom from those, who would not
at a feast
Leave one poor apple for thy love *l*
0 show thyself, &e.
  He did, he came: 0 my Redeemer
dear,
After all this canst thou be strange?
  So many years baptized, and not ap-
pear;
As if thy love could fail or change?
0 show thyself, &c.

Yet if thou stayest still, why must I
stay?
My God, what is this world to me?
This world of woe? Hence, all ye
clouds, away,
Away; I must get up and see.
0 show thyself, &e.
  What is this weary world; this meat
and drink,
That chains us by the teeth so fast *l*
  What is this woman-kind, which I
can wink
Into a blackness and distaste?
0 show thyself, &e.
  With one small sigh thou gavest me
th' other day I blasted all the joys about
me:
  And scowling on them as they pined
away,
  Now come again, said I, and flout
me.
0 show thyself, &c.
  Nothing but drought and dearth, but
bush and brake, Which way soe'er I
look, I see.
Some may dream merrily, but when
they wake,
  They dress themselves and come to
thee.
0 show thyself, &e.
Wc talk of harvests; there arc no such
things,
But when we leave our corn and hay:
  There is no fruitful year, but that
which brings
The last and loved, though dreadful day.
0 show thyself, &e.
0 loose this frame, this knot of man un-
tie, That my free soul may use her wing,
  Which now is pinion'd with mortali-
ty, As an entangled, hamper'd tiling. 0
show thyself, &e.
  What have I left, that I should stay
and groan?
The most of me to heaven is fled:
My thoughts and joys arc all pack'd up
and gone,
And for their old acquaintance plead.
0 show thyself, &e.
  Come, dearest Lord, pass not this
holy season,
  My flesh and bones and joints do
pray: And even my verse, when by the
rhyme and reason The word is *Stay,*
says ever, *Gome.* 0 show thyself to me,

Or take me up to thee!
THE BRITISH CHURCH.
I Joy, dear Mother, when I view
Thy perfect lineaments and hue
  Both sweet and bright:
Beauty in thee takes up her place,
And dates her letters from thy face,
  When she doth write.
  A fine aspect in fit array,
Neither too mean, nor yet too gay,
Shows who is best:
Outlandish looks may not compare;
For all they cither painted are,
  Or else undrest.
  She on the hills, which wantonly
Allureth all in hope to be
By her preferr'd,
  Hath kiss'd so long her painted
shrines, That even her face by kissing
shines, For her reward.
  She in the valley is so shy
  Of dressing, that her hair doth lie
About her cars: While she avoids her
neighbour's pride, She wholly goes on
th' other side,
  And nothing wears.
  But, dearest Mother (what those
miss),
The mean thy praise and glory is,
And long may be.
Blessed be God, whose love it was
To double-moat thee with his grace,
  And none but thee.
THE QUIP.
The merry world did on a day
With his train-bands and mates agree
To meet together, where I lay,
And all in sport to jeer at me.
  First, Beauty crept into a Rose;
Which when I pluck'd not, Sir, said she,
Tell me, I pray, whose hands arc those?
But thou shalt answer, Lord, for me.
  Then Money came, and chinking
still,
What tune is this, poor man? said he:
I heard in Music you had skill:
But thou shall answer, Lord, for me.
  Then came bravo Glory puffing by
In silks that whistled, who but ho!
He scarce allow'd me half an eye:
But thou shall answer, Lord, for me.
  Then came quick Wit and Conversa-
tion,
And he would needs a comfort be,
And, to be short, make an oration.

But thou shall answer, Lord, for me.

Yet when the hour of thy design
To answer these fine things shall come;
Speak not at large, say, I am thine,
And then they have their answer home.

VANITY.

Poor silly soul, whose hope and head
lies low;
Whose flat delights on earth do creep
and grow:
To whom the stars shine not so fair, as
eyes;
Nor solid work, as false embroideries;
Hark and beware, lest what you now do
measure,
And write for sweet, prove a most sour
displeasure.
0 hear betimes, lest thy relenting
May come to late!
To purchase heaven for repenting
Is no hard rate.
If souls be made of earthly mould,
Let them lovo gold;
If born on high,
Let them unto their kindred fly:
For they can never be at rest,
Till they regain their ancient nest.

Then silly soul, take heed; for earthly
joy.

Is but a bubble, and makes thee a boy.

THE DAWNING.

Awake, sad heart,-whom sorrow ever
drowns: Take up thine eyes, which feed
on earth,
Unfold thy forehead gather'd into
frowns:
Thy Saviour comes, and with him
mirth:
Awake, awake;
And with a thankful heart his comforts
take.
. But thou dost still lament, and pine,
and cry;
And feel his death, but not his victory.

Arise, sad heart; if thou dost not withstand, Christ's resurrection thine may
be:
Do not by hanging down break from the
hand,

Which, as it riscth, raiscth thee:

Arise, arise; And with his burial-linen
dry thine eyes.

Christ left his grave-clothes, that we
might, when grief

Draws tears, or blood, not want a

handkerchief.

JESU.

Jesu is in my heart, his sacred name
Is deeply carved there: but the other
week
A great affliction broke the little frame,
Even all to pieces; which I went to seek:
h

And first I found the corner where
Mas J,
After, where ES, and next where U was
graved.
"When I had got these parcels, instantly
I sat mo down to spell them, and per-
ceived
That to my broken heart he was / *ease
you,*
And to my whole is *JESU.*

BUSINESS.

Caxst be idle? canst thou play,
Foolish soul who sinn'd to-day?

Rivers run, and springs each one
Know their home, and get them gone:
I last thou tears, or hast thou none?

If, poor soul, thou hast no tears,
Would thou hadst no faults or fears!
Who hath these, those ills forbears.

Winds still work: it is their plot,
Be the season cold or hot:
Hast thou sighs, or hast thou not?

If thou hast no sighs or groans,
Would thou hadst no flesh and bones I
Lesser pains 'scape greater ones.

But if yet thou idle be,
Foolish soul, who died for thee /
Who did leave his Father's throne,
To assume thy flesh and bone?
Had ho life, or had he none?

If he had not lived for thee,
Thou hadst died most wretchedly;
And two deaths had been thy fee.
lie so far thy good did plot,
That his own self he forgot.
Did he die, or did he not?

If he had not died for thee,
Thou hadst lived in misery.
Two lives worse than ten deaths be.

And hath any space of breath
'Twixt his sins and Saviour's death /
lie that loscth gold, though dross,
Tells to all he meets, his cross:
He that sins, hath he no loss?
lie that finds a silver vein,
Thinks on it, and thinks again:
Brings thy Saviour's death no gain?

"Who in heart not ever kneels,
Neither sin nor Saviour feels.

DIALOGUE.

Sweetest Saviour, if my soul
Were but worth the having,
Quickly should I then control
Any. thought of waving.

But when all my care and pains
Cannot give the name of gains
To thy wretch so full of stains;
What delight or hope remains?
Wliat (Child), is the balance thine t
Thine the poise and measure?
If I say, Thou shalt be mine,
Finger not my treasure.
What the gains in having thee
Do amount to, only he,
Who for man was sold, can see,
That trans/err d the accounts to me.

But as I can see no merit, Leading to
this favour:
So the way to fit me for it,
Is beyond my savour.
As the reason then is thine;
So the way is none of mine:
I disclaim the whole design:
Sin disclaims and I resign.
That is all, if that I coidd Get without re-
pining;
And my clay my creature xuould
Follow my resigning:
That as I did freely part
With my glory and desert,
Left all joys to feel all smart

Ah I no more: thou brcak'st my heart.

DULNESS.

Why do I languish thus, drooping and
dull, As if I were all earth?
0 give me quickness, that I may with
mirth
Praise thee brimful!

The wanton lover in a curious strain
Can praise his fairest fair;JU-U. "4
And with quaint metaphors her curled
hair

Curl o'er again: '£

Thou art my loveliness, my life, my
light, bWuu/"

Beauty alone to mc:-- uoXj

Thy bloody death and undeserved,
makes thee,
Pure red and white. uVj--H

When all perfections as but ond appear,-/ urf That those thy form doth
show,

The very dust, where thou dost tread and go,
Makes beauties here;
    Where arc my lines then? my approaches? views?
Where arc my window-songs /
Lovers arc still pretending, and even wrongs
Sharpen their Muse.
But I am lost in flesh, whose sugar'd lies
Still mock me, and grow bold:
Sure thou didst put a mind there, if I could
Find where it lies.
    Lord, clear thy gift, that vithaT6h-stant wit/'
    I may but look towards thee: *Look* only; for to *love* thee, who can be, What angel, fit / LOVE-JOY.

    As on a window late 1 cast mine eye,
I saw a vine drop grapes with J and C
Anncal'd on every bunch. One standing by
Ask'd what it meant. 1 (who am never loth
To spend my judgment) said, it scem'd to mo
To be the body and the letters both
Of *Joy* and *Charity.* Sir, you have not miss'd,
The man replied; It figures Jesus CmuyT.
. TltOVIDENCE.
0 Sacked Providence, who from end to end
Strongly and sweetly movest! shall I write,
And not of thee, through whom my fingers bend
To hold my quill / shall they not do thee right /
Of all the creatures both in sea and land,
Only to Alan thou hast made known thy ways,
And put the pen alone into his hand,
And made him Secretary of thy praise.
    Beasts fain would sing; birds ditty to their notes;
Trees would be tuning on their native lute
To thy renown: but all their hands and throats
Are brought to Man, while they arc lame and mute.

Man is the world's High Priest: he doth present
    The sacrifice for all; while they below
    Unto the service mutter an assent,
    Such as springs use that fall, and winds that blow.
lie that to praise and laud thcc doth refrain,
Doth not refrain unto himself alone,
But robs a thousand who would praise thee fain;
And doth commit a world of sin in one.
The beasts say, Eat me; but, if beasts must teach,
The tongue is yours to cat, but mine to praise.
The trees say, Pull me: but the hand you stretch
Is mine to write, as it is jours to raise.
    Wherefore, most sacred Spirit, I here present
For me and all my fellows praise to thee:
And just it is that I should pay the rent,
Because the benefit accrues to me.
    We all acknowledge both thy power and love
To be exact, transcendent, and divine;
Who dost so strongly and so sweetly move,
While all things have their will, yet none but thine.
    For either thy *command,* or thy *permission*
Lay hands on all: they are thy *rhjht* and *left:*
The first puts on with speed and expedition;
The other curbs sin's stealing pace and theft;
    Nothing escapes them both: all must appear,
And be disposed, and dress'd, and tuned by thee,
Who sweetly tempcr'st all. If we could hear
Thy skill and art, what music would it be!
    Thou art in small things great, not small in any:
Thy even praise can neither rise nor fall.
Thou art in all things one, in each thing many:
For thou art infinite in one and all.

    Tempests arc calm to thee, they know thy hand,
And hold it fast, as children do their father's,
Which cry and follow. Thou hast made poor sand
Check the proud sea, even when it swells and gathers.
    Thy cupboard serves the world: the meat is set
Where all may reach: no beast but knows his feed.
Birds teach us hawking: fishes have their net:
The great prey on the less, they on somc weed.
    Nothing engendcr'd doth prevent his meat;
Flies have their table spread, ere they appear;
Some creatures have in winter what to cat;
Others do sleep, and envy not their cheer.
    How finely dost thou times and seasons spin,
And make a twist checker'd with night and day!
Which as it lengthens, winds, and winds us in,
As bowls go on, but turning all the way.
    Each creature hath a wisdom for his good.
The pigeons feed their tender offspring crying,
When they arc callow; but withdraw their food,
When they arc Hedged, that need may teach them flying.
    Bees work for man; and yet they never bruise
Their master's flower, but leave it, having done,
As fair as ever, and as fit to use:
So both the flower doth stay, and honey run.
    Sheep cat the grass, and dung thc ground for more:
Trees after bearing drop their leaves for soil:
Springs vent their streams, and by expense get store:
Clouds cool by heat, and baths by cooling boil.
    Who hath the virtue to express the

rare
And curious virtues both of herbs and stones?
Is there an herb for that? 0 that thy caro
Would show a root, that gives expressions I
  And if an herb hath power, what have the stars?
A rose, besides his beauty, is a cure.
Doubtless our plagues and plenty, peace and wars,
Arc there much surer than our art is sure.
  Thou hast hid metals: man may take them thence;
I5ut at his peril: when he digs the place,
lie makes a grave: as if the thing had sense,
And thrcaten'd man, that he should fill the space.
  Even poisons praise thee. Should a thing be lost?
Should creatures want, for want of heed, their due?
Since whore are poisons, antidotes arc most;
The help stands close, and keeps the fear in view.
  The sea, which seems to stop the traveller,
Is by a ship the speedier passage made.
The winds, who think they rule the mariner,
Arc ruled by him, and taught to serve his trade.
  And as thy house is full, so I adore
Thy curious art in marshalling thy goods
  The hills with health abound, the vales with store;
  The South with marble; North with furs and woods.
  Hard things arc glorious; easy things good cheap;
The common all men have; that which is rare,
Men therefore seek to have, and care to keep.
The healthy frosts with summer-fruits compare.
  Light without wind is glass: warm without weight
Is wool and furs: cool without closeness, shade:
Speed without pains, a horse: tall without height,
A servile hawk: low without loss, a spade.
  All countries have enough to serve their need:
If they seek fine things, thou dost make them run
For their offence; and then dost turn their speed
To be commerce and trade from sun to sun.
  Nothing wears clothes, but Man; nothing doth need
But he to wear them. Nothing useth fire,
I3ut Man alone, to show his heavenly breed:
And only he hath fuel in desire.
  "When th' earth was dry, thou madest a sea of wet:
When that lay gathcr'd, thou didst broach the. mountains:
"When yet some places could no moisture get,
The winds grew gardeners, and the clouds good fountains.
  Rain, do not hurt my flowers; but gently spend
Your honey drops: press not to smell them here;
"When they arc ripe, their odour will ascend,
And at your lodging with their thanks appear.
  How harsh arc thorns to pears! and yet they make
A better hedge, and need less reparation.
How smooth arc silks, compared with a stake,
Or with a stone! yet make no good foundation.
  Sometimes thou dost divide thy gifts to man,
Sometimes unite. The Indian nut alone
Is clothing, meat and trencher, drink and can,
Boat, cable, sail and needle, all in one.
  Most herbs that grow in brooks, arc hot and dry.
Cold fruit's warm kernels help against the wind.
The lemon's juice and rind cure mutually.
The whey of milk doth loose, the milk doth bind.

Thy creatures leap not, but express a feast,
AVhcrc all the guests sit close, and nothing wants.
Frogs marry fish and flesh; bats, bird and beast;
Sponges, nonsense and sense; mines, th' earth and plants.
  To show thou art not bound, as if thy lot
Were worse than ours, sometimes thou shiftest hands.
Most things move th' undcr-jaw; the Crocodile not.
Most things sleep lying, th' Elephant leans or stands.
  But who hath praise enough? nay, who hath any I
None can express thy works, but he that knows them;
And none can know thy works, which are so many,
And so complete, but only he that owes them.
  All things that are, though thev have several ways,
Yet in their being join with one advice
To honour thee: and so I give thee praise
In all my other hymns, but in this twice.
  Each thing that is, although in use and name
It go for one, hath many ways in store
To honour thee; and so each hymn thy fame
Extolleth many ways, yet this one more.
HOPE.
  I GAVE to Hope a Watch of mine: but ho An Anchor gave to me.
Then an old Prayer-book I did present:
  And he an Optic sent.
  With that I gave a Phial full of tears:
But he a few green cars.
  Ah, loiterer! I'll no more, no more I'll bring:
I did expect a Ring.
SINS ROUND.
  Sorry I am, my God, sorry I am,
  That my offences course it in a ring.
  My thoughts arc working like a busy flame,
  Until their Cockatrice they hatch and bring:
  And when they once have perfected their draughts,

My words take fire from my inflamed thoughts.

My words take fire from my inflamed thoughts,
Which spit it forth like the Sicilian hill.
They vent the wares, and pass them with their faults,
And by their breathing ventilate the ill.
But words suffice not, where arc lewd intentions:
My hands do join to finish the inventions:
My hands do join to finish the inventions:
And so my sins ascend three storeys high,
As Babel grew, before there were dissensions.
Yet ill deeds loiter not: for they supply
New thoughts of sinning; wherefore, to my shame,
Sorry I am, my God, sorry I am.

TIME.

Meeting with Time, Slack thing, said I,
    Thy scythe is dull; whet it for shame.
    No marvel, Sir, he did reply,
    If it at length deserve some blame:
    But where one man would have me grind it,
Twenty for one too sharp do find it.
    Perhaps some such of old did pass,
    Who above all things loved this life;
    To whom thy scythe a hatchet was,
    Which now is but a pruning-knife.
    Christ's coming hath made Man thy debtor.
Since by thy cutting he grows better.
    And in his blessing thou art blest:
    For where thou only wert before
    An executioner at best,
    Thou art a gardener now, and more.
An usher to convey our souls
Beyond the utmost stars and poles.
    And this is that makes life so lonr,
While it detains us from our God.
Even pleasures here increase the wrong:
And length of days lengthen the rod.
    Who wants the place, where God doth dwell,
    Partakes already half of hell.
    Of what strange length must that needs be,

Which even eternity excludes!
Thus far Time heard me patiently:
Then chafing said, This man deludes:
    What do I here before his door?
    He doth not crave less time, but more.

GRATEFULNESS.

Thou that hast given so much to me,
Give one thing more, a grateful heart.
See how thy beggar works on thee
    By art.
    He makes thy gifts occasion more,
And says, If ho in this bo crost,
All thou hast given him heretofore
    Is lost.
    But thou didst reckon, when at first
Thy word our hearts and hands did crave,
What it would come to at the worst
    To save.
    Perpetual knockings at thy door.
Tears sullying thy transparent rooms,
Gift upon gift; much would have more,
    And comes.
    This notwithstanding, thou went'st on,
And didst allow us all our noise:
Nay, thou hast made a sigh and groan
    Thy joys.
    Not that thou hast not still above
Much better tunes, than groans can make;
But that these country-airs thy love
    Did take.
    Wherefore I cry, and cry again;
And in no quiet canst thou be,
Till I a thankful heart obtain
    Of thee:
    Not thankful, when it pleascth rue:
As if thy blessings had spare days:
But such a heart, whose pulse may be
    Thy praise.

PEACE.

Sweet Peace, where dost thou dwell? I humbly crave,
Let me once know.
I sought thec in a secret cave,
And ask'd, if Peace were there.
A hollow wind did seem to answer, No:
Go seek elsewhere.
    I did; and going did a rainbow note:
Surely, thought I,
This is the lace of Peace's coat:
I will search out the matter.
But while I look'd, the clouds immediately

Did break and scatter.
    Then went I to a garden, and did spy
A gallant flower,
The Crown Imperial: Sure, said I,
Peace at the root must dwell.
But when I digg'd, I saw a worm devour
What show'd so well.
    At length 1 met a reverend good old man:
Whom when for Pcaco
I did demand, he thus began:
There was a Prince of old
At Salem dwelt, who lived with good increase
Of flock and fold.
    He sweetly lived; yet sweetness did not save
His life from foes.
But after death out of his grave
There sprang twelve stalks of wheat:
Which many wondering at, got some of those
To plant and set.
    It prospcr'd strangely, and did soon disperse
Through all the earth:
For they that taste it do rehearse,
That virtue lies therein;
A secret virtue, bringing peace and mirth
By flight of sin.
    Take of this grain, which in my garden grows,
And grows for you;
Make bread of it: and that repose
And peace, which every where
With so much earnestness you do pursue,
Is only there.

CONFESSION.

Oh, what a cunning guest
Is this same grief! within my heart I made
Closets; and in them many a chest; And like a master in my trade,
In those chests, boxes; in each box, a till:
Yet grief knows all, and enters when he will.
    No screw, no piercer can
    Into a piece of timber work and wind,
As God's afflictions into man,
When he a torture hath design'd.
    They are too subtle for the subtlest hearts;

And faU, like rheums, upon the tend-crest parts.

We are the earth; and they, Like moles within us, heave, and cast about:

And till they foot and clutch their prey, They never cool, much less give out. No Smith can make such locks, but they have keys; Closets arc I Ialls to them; and hearts, highways.

Only an open breast

Doth shut them out, so that they cannot enter;

Or, if they cuter, cannot rest,

But quickly seek some new adventure.

Smooth open hearts no fastening have; but fiction.

Doth give a hold and handle to affliction.

Wherefore my faults and sins, Lord, I acknowledge; take thy plagues away:

I For since confession pardon wins,

I challenge here the brightest day,

The clearest diamond: let them do their best,

They shall be thick and cloudy to my breast.

GIDDINESS.

Oh, what a thing is Man! how far from power,

From settled peace and rest! Ho is some twenty several men at least Each several hour.

One while he counts of heaven, as of his treasure:

But then a thought creeps in, And calls him coward, who for fear of sin Will lose a pleasure.

Now he will fight it out, and to the wars;

Now cat his bread in peace, And snudgo in quiet: now he scorns increase; Now all day spares.

Ho builds a house, which quickly down must go,

As if a whirlwind blew And crush'd the building: and 'tis partly true, His mind is so.

Oh, what a sight were Man, if his attires

Did alter with his mind; And, like a Dolphin's skin, his clothes combined With his desires!

Surely if each one saw another's heart,

There would be no commerce,

No Sale or Bargain pass: all would disperse,

And live apart.

Lord, mend or rather make us: one creation Will not suffice our turn:

Except thou make us daily, we shall spurn

Our own salvation.

THE BUNCH OF GRAPES.

Joy, I did lock thee up: but some bad man

Hath let thee out aain:

And now, methinks, I am whereI began

Seven years ago: one vogue and vein,

One air of thoughts usurps my brain

I did toward Canaan draw; but now I am

Brought back to the Itcd Sea, the sea of shame.

For as the Jews of old by God's command

Travell'd, and saw no town;

So now each Christian hath his journejs spann'd:

Their story pens and sets us down.

A single deed is small renown.

God's works arc wide, and let in future times;

His ancient justice overflows our crimes.

Then have we too our guardian fires and clouds;

Our Scripture-dcw drops fast: tte have our sands and serpents, tents and shrouds;

Alas! our murmurings come not last.

But wherc's the cluster? wherc's the taste

Of mine inheritance? Lord, if I must borrow,

Let mo as well take up their joy, as sorrow.

But can he want the grape, who hath the wine I

I have their fruit, and more. Blessed bo God, who prospcr'd *Noah's* vine,

And made it bring forth grapes good store.

But much more Him I must adore,

Who of the law's sour juice sweet wine did make,

Even God himself, being pressed for my sake.

LOVE UNKNOWN.

Dear friend, sit down, the tale is long and sad:

And in my faintings I presume your love

Will more comply, than help. A Lord I had,

And have, of whom some grounds, which may improve,

I hold for two lives, and both lives in me.

To him I brought a dish of fruit one day,

And in the middle placed my heart. But he (I sigh to say) Look'd on a servant, who did know his eye Better than you know me, or (which is one) Than I myself. The servant instantly Quitting the fruit, seized on my heart alono And threw it in a font, wherein did fall A stream of blood, which issued from the side Of a great rock: I well remember all, And have good cause: there it was dipt and dyed, And wash'd, aud wrung: the very wringing yet En forccth tears. *Your heart was foul, I fear.* Indeed 'tis true. I did and do commit Many a fault more than my lease will bear;

Yet still ask'd pardon, and was not denied.

But you shall hear. After my heart was well,

And clean and fair, as I one even-tide (I sigh to tell)

Walk'd by myself abroad, I saw a large And spacious furnace flaming, and thereon

A boiling caldron, round about whose verge

"Was in great letters set Affliction.

The greatness show'd the owner. So I went

To fetch a sacrifice out of my fold,

Thinking with that, which I did thus present,

To warm his love, which I did fear grew cold.

But as my heart did tender it, the man "Who was to take it from me, slipt his hand,

And threw my heart into the scalding pan;

My heart, that brought it (do you understand?),

The offerer's heart. *Your heart was hard, J fear.*

Indeed 'tis true. I found a callous matter
Began to spread and to expatiate there:
But with a richer drug, than scalding water,
I bathed it often, even with holy blood,
Which at a board, while many drank bare wine,
A friend did steal into my cup for good,
Even taken inwardly, and most divine
To supple hardnesses. But at the length
Out of the caldron getting, soon I fled
Unto my house, where to repair the strength
"Which I had lost, I hasted to my bed:
But when I thought to sleep out all these faults,
(I sigh to speak)
I found that some had stufT'd the bed with thoughts,
I would say *thorns.* Dear, could my heart not break,
When with my pleasures even my rest was gone?
Full well I understood, who had been there:
    For I had given the key to none, but one:
It must be he. *Your heart was dull, I fear.*
Indeed a slack and sleepy stato of mind
Did oft possess me, so that when I pray'd,
Though my lips went, my heart did stay behind.
But all my scores were by another paid,
Who took the debt upon him. *Truly, Friend,*
For ought I hear, your Master shows to you
More favour than you wot of. Mark the end.
The Font did only, what was old, renew:
The Caldron suppled, what was groivn too hard:
The Thorns did quicken, what ivas grown too dull:
All did but strive tj mend, what you had marr'd.
Wiercfore be cheer d, and praise him to the full
Each day, each hour, each moment of the week,
Who fain would have you be, new, tender, quick.
MAN'S MEDLEY.

Hark, how the birds do sing,
And woods do ring.
All creatures have their joy, and man hath his.
Yet if we rightly measure,
Man's joy and pleasure
Rather hereafter, than in present, is.
To this life things of sense
    Make their pretence: In tb' other Angels have a right by birth:. Man ties them both alone,
    And makes them one, With th' one hand touching heaven, with the other earth. In soul he mounts and flies, Jn flesh he dies. lie wears a stuff whose thread is coarse and round, But trinun'd with curious lace, And should take place After the trimming, not the stuff and ground.
Not, that he may not here
Taste of the cheer:
But as birds drink, and straight lift up their head;
So must he sip, and think
Of better drink lie may attain to, after he is dead.
But as his joys arc double,
So is his trouble.
Ho hath two winters, other things but one:
Both frosts and thoughts do nip,
And bite his lip;
And ho of all things fears two deaths alone.
o
Yet even the greatest griefs May be reliefs, Could he but take them right, and in their ways. Happy is he, whose heart I lath found the art To turn his double pains to double praise.
THE STORM.
If as the winds and waters here below
Do fly and flow,
My sighs and tears as busy were above;
Sure they would move
And much affect thee, as tempestuous times
Amaze poor mortals, and object their crimes.
    Stars have their storms, even in a high degree, As well as we.
A throbbing conscience spurred by remorse
Hath a strange force:
It quits the earth, and mounting more

and more,
Dares to assault thee, and besiege thy door.
    There it stands knocking, to thy music's wrong,
    And drowns the song. Glory and honour arc set by till it
    An answer get. Poets have wrong'd poor storms: such days arc best; They purge the air without, within the breast.
PARADISE.
I Bless thee, Lord, because I Grow
Among thy trees, which in a Row
To thee both fruit and order ow.
    What open force, or hidden Charm
Can blast my fruit, or bring me Harm,
While the enclosure is thine Arm?
    Enclose mo still, for fear I Start.
Be to mo rather sharp and Tart,
Than let mo want thy hand and Art.
    When thou dost greater judgments sP.RE,: And with thy knife but prune and PARE, Even fruitful trees more fruitful ARE.
    Such sharpness shows the sweetest Friend: Such cuttings rather heal than Rend: And such beginnings touch their End. THE METHOD.
Poor heart, lament,
For since thy God rcfuscth still,
There is some rub, some discontent,
Which cools his will.
Thy Father *could*
Quickly effect, what thou dost move;
For he is *Power:* and sure he *would;*
For he is *Love.*
    Co search this thing. Tumble thy breast, and turn thy book If thou hadst lost a "love or ring,
    Wouldst thou not look?
What do I sec
Written above there? *Yesterday*
I did behave me carelessly,
When I did pray. And should God's car
To such inditlcrents chained be.
Who do not their own motions hear?
Is God less free *I* But stay! what's there?
Late when I would have something done,
I had a motion to forbear.
Yet I went on. And should God's car,
Which needs not man, be tied to those
Who hear not him, but quickly hear
    His utter foes?

Then once more pray:
Down with thy knees, up with thy voice:
Seek pardon first, and God will say,
Glad heart, rejoice. DIVINITY.
As men, for fear the stars should sleep and nod,
And trip at night, have spheres supplied;
As if a star were duller than a clod,
Which knows his way without a guide:
Just so the other heaven they also serve, Divinity's transcendent sky:
Which with the edge of wit they cut and carve.
Reason triumphs, and Faith lies by.
Could not that wisdom, which first broach'd the wine,
Have thicken'd it with definitions?
And jagg'd his seamless coat, had that been fine,
With curious questions and divisions?
But.ill the doctrine,-which he taught and gave,
Was clear as heaven, from whence it came.
At least those beams of truth, which only save,
Surpass in brightness any flame.
Love God, and love your neighbour. Watch and pray. Do as you, would be dune nnlo. 0 dark instructions, even as dark as day!
Who can these Gordian knots undo *l*
But he doth bid us take his blood for wine.
Bid what ho please; yet I am sure,
To take and taste what he doth there design,
Is all that saves, and not obscure.
Then burn thy Epicycles, foolish man;
Break all thy spheres, and save thy head; Faith needs no staff" of flesh, but stoutly can
To Heaven alone both go, and lead.
EPIIESIANS IV. 30.
" CIRIEVE NOT THE HOLY SPIRIT," ETC.
And art thou grieved, sweet and sacred Dove,
When I am sour,
And cross thy love *l*
Grieved for me *l* the God of strength and power
Grieved for a worm, which when I

tread,
I pass away and leave it dead *l*
Then weep, mine eyes, the God of love doth grieve:
Weep foolish heart,
And weeping live;
For death is dry as dust. Yet if we part,
End as the night, whose sable hue
Your sins express; melt into dew.
When saucy Mirth shall knock or call at door,
Cry out, Oct hence,
Or cry no more.
Almighty God doth grieve, he puts on sense:
I sin not to my grief alone,
But to my God's too; he doth groan.
0 take thy lute, and tunc it to a strain,
Which may with thee
All day complain.
There can no discord but in ceasing bo.
Marbles can weep; and surely strings
More bowels have, than such hard things.
Lord, I adjudge myself to tears and grief,
Even endless tears
Without relief.
If a clear spring for me no time forbears,
But runs, although I be not dry;
I am no Crystal, what shall I?
Yet if I wail not still, since still to wail
Nature denies;
And flesh would fail,
If my deserts were masters of mine eyes:
Lord, pardon, for thy Son makes good
My want of tears with store of blood.
THE FAMILY.
What doth this noise of thoughts within my heart,
As if they had a part *l*
What do these loud complaints and pulling fears,
As if there Merc no rule or cars?
But, Lord, the house and family arc thine,
Though some of them repine.
Turn out these wranglers, which defile thy scat:
For where thou dwcllest all is neat.
First Peace and Silence all disputes control, Then Order plays the soul;

And giving all things their set forms and hours,
Makes of wild woods sweet walks and bowers.
Humble Obedience near the door doth stand, Expecting a command:
Than whom in waiting nothing seems more slow,
Nothing more quick when she doth go.
Joys oft arc there, and griefs as oft as joys; But griefs without a noise:
Yet speak they louder, than distempcr'd fears:
What is so shrill as sileut tears *l*
This is thy house, with these it doth abound:
And where these arc not found,
Perhaps thou comest sometimes, and for a day;
But not to make a constant stay.
TUB SIZE.
Content thce, greedy heart.
Modest and moderate joys to those, that have
Title to more hereafter when they part,
Arc passing brave.
Let th' upper springs into the low
Descend and fall, and thou dost flow.
What though some have a fraught
Of cloves and nutmegs, and in cinnamon sail *l*
If thou hast wherewithal to spice a draught,
When griefs prevail,
And for the future time art heir
To th' Isle of Spices, is't not fair?
To be in both worlds full
Is more than God was, who was hungry here.
Wouldst thou his laws of fasting disannul?
Enact good cheer *l*
Lay out thy joy, yet hope to save it?
Wouldst thou both cat thy cake, and have it
Great joys arc all at once; But little do reserve themselves for more: Those have their hopes; these what they have renounce, And live on score: Those arc at home; these journey still, And meet the rest on *Sioris* hill.
Thy Saviour sentenced joy, And in the flesh condemn'd it as unfit,
At least in lump: for such cloth oft destroy;

Whereas a bit
Doth 'ticc us on to hopes of more,
And for the present health restore.
A Christian's state and case
Is not a corpulent, but a thin and spare,
Yet active strength: whose long and
bony face
Content and care
Do seem to equally divide,
Like a pretender, not a bride.
  Wherefore sit down, good heart;
  Grasp not at much, for fear thou los-
est all.
  If comforts fell according to desert,
  They would great frosts and snows
destroy:
For we should count, Since the last joy.
Then close again the scam,
Which thou hast open'd; do not spread
thy robe
In hope of great things. Call to mind thy
dream,
An earthly globe,
On whose meridian was engraven,
*These Seas are tears, and Heaven the
haven.*
ARTILLERY.
  As I one evening sat before my cell,
Mcthought a star did shoot into my lap.
I rose, and shook my clothes, as know-
ing well,
That from small fires comes oft no
small mishap
When suddenly I heard one say,
Do as thou usest, disobey,
Expel good motions from thy breast,
*Which have tlieface of fire, but end in
rest.*
  I, who had heard of music in the
spheres,
But not of speech in stars, began to
muse:
But turning to my God, whose ministers
The stars and all things arc; If I refuse,
Dread Lord, said I, so oft my good;
Then I refuse not even with blood
To wash away my stubborn thought:
For I will do, or suffer what I ought.
  But I have also stars and shooters too,
Born where thy servants both artilleries
use.
My tears and prayers night and day do
woo,
And work up to thee; yet thou dost
refuse.

Not but I am (I must say still)
Much more obliged to do thy will,
Than thou to grant mine: but because
Thy promise now hath even set thee thy
laws.
  Then wc arc shooters both, and thou
dost deign
To enter combat with us, and contest
With thine own clay. But I would parley
fain:
Shun not my arrows, and behold my
breast.
  Yet if thou shuunest, I am thine:
  I must be so, if I am mine.
  There is no articling with thee: I am
but finite, yet thine infinitely.
CIIURCII-REXTS AND SCHISMS.
Brave rose, (alas!) where art thou? in
the chair,
Where thou didst lately so triumph and
shine,
A worm doth sit, whose many feet and
hair
Arc the more foul, the more thou vert
divine.
This, this hath done it, this did bite the
root
And bottom of the leaves: which when
the wind
Did once perceive, it blew them under
foot,
Where rude unhallow'd steps do crush
and grind
Their beauteous glories. Only shreds of
thee,
And those all bitten, in thy chair I see.
  Why doth my Mother blush? is she
the rose,
And shows it so / Indeed Christ's pre-
cious blood
Gave you a colour once; which when
your foes
Thought to let out, the bleeding did you
good.
And made you look much fresher than
before.
But when debates and fretting jeal-
ousies
Did worm and work within you more
and more,
Your colour faded, and calamities
  Turned your ruddy into pale and
bleak:
Your health and beauty both began to
break.

Then did your several parts unloose
and start:
Which when your neighbours saw. like
a north wind
They rushed in, and cast them in the dirt
Where Pagans tread. 0 Mother dear and
kind,
Where shall I get me eyes enough to
weep,
As many eyes as stars / since it is night,
And much of *Asia* and *Europe* fast
asleep,
And even all *A/rick;* would at least I
might
With these two poor ones lick up all the
dew.
Which falls by night, and pour it out for
you!
  K JUSTICE.
0 Dbeadful Justice, what a fright and
terror
Wast thou of old,
When Sin and Error
Did show and shape thy looks to me,
And through their glass discolour thee!
He that did but look up, Mas proud and
bold.
The dishes of thy balancc seem'd to
gape,
  Like two great pits;
  The beam and scape
  Did like some tottering engine show:
  Thy hand above did burn and glow,
  Daunting the stoutest hearts, the
proudest wits.
  But now that Christ's pure veil pre-
sents the sight,
I see no fears:
Thy hand is white,
Thy scales like buckets, which attend
And interchangeably descend,
Lifting to heaven from this well of tears.
  For where before thou still didst call
on me,
Now I still touch
And harp on thee.
God's promises have made thee mine:
Why should I justice now decline /
Against me there is none, but for me
much.
THE PILGRIMAGE.
  I TRAVELl/D on, seeing the hill,
where lay
My expectation.
A long it was and weary way.

The gloomy cave of Desperation
I left on the one, and on the other side
The rock of Pride.

And so I came to Fancy's meadow strew'd
With many a flower:
Fain would I here have made abode,
But I was quicken'd by the hour.
So to Care's copse I came, and there got through
With much ado.

That led me to the wild of Passion; which
Some call the wold;
A wasted place, but sometimes rich.
Here I was robb'd of all my gold,
Save one good Angel, which a friend had tied
Close to my side.

At length I got unto the gladsome hill,
Where lay my hope,
Where lay my heart; and climbing still,
When I had gain'd the brow and top,
A lake of brackish waters on the ground
Was all I found.

With that abash'd and stmck with many a sting
Of swarming fears,
I fell, and cried, Alas! my King;
Can both the way and end be tears?
Yet taking heart I rose, and then perceived
I was deceived:

My hill was further: so I flung away,
Yet heard a cry
Just as I went, *None goes that way
And lives:* If that be all, said I,
After so foul a journey death is fair,
And but a chair.

THE HOLD-FAST.

I Threaten'd to observe the strict decree
Of my dear God with all my power and might: But I was told by one, it could not be;
Yet I might trust in God to be my light.

Then will I trust; said I, in him alone.
Nay, even to trust in him, was also his:
We must confess, that nothing is our own.

Then I confess that he my succour is:
But to have nought is ours, not to confess

That we have nought. I stood amazed at this, Much troubled, till I heard a friend express,
That all things were more ours by being his.

What *Adam* had, and forfeited for all, *Christ* keepcth now, who cannot fail or fall.

COMPLAINING.

Do not beguile my heart, Because thou art My power and wisdom. Put me not to shame. Because I am Thy clay that weeps, thy dust that calls.

Thou art the Lord of glory; The deed and story Arc both thy due: but I a silly fly, That live or die, According as the weather falls.

Art thou all justice, Lord?
Shows not thy word
More attributes? Am I all throat or eye,
To weep or cry?
Nave I no parts but those of grief?
Let not thy wrathful power Afflict my hour,
My inch of life: or let thy gracious power
Contract my hour,
That I may climb and find relief.

THE DISCHARGE.

Busy inquiring heart, what wouldst thou know?
Why dost thou pry,
And turn, and leer, and with a licorous eye
Look high and low;
And in thy lookings stretch and grow?
Hast thou not made thy counts, and summ'd up all *l* Did not thy heart
Give up the whole, and with the whole depart?
Let what will fall:
That which is past who can recall *l*

Thy life is God's, thy time to come is gone, And is his right.
He is thy night at noon: he is at night Thy noon alone.
The crop is his, for ho.hath sown.
And well it was for thee, when this befell,
That God did make
Thy business his, and in thy life partake:
For thou canst tell,
If it bo his once, all is well.

Only the present is thy part and fee.

And happy thou,
If, though thou didst not beat thy future brow,
Thou couldst well sec
What present things required of thee.
They ask enough; why shouklst thou further go 1 Raise not the mud
Of future depths, but drink the clear and good..
Dig not for woe
In times to come; for it will grow.

Man and the present fit: if he provide,
He breaks the square.
This hour is mine: if for the next I care,
I grow too wide,
And do encroach upon death's side.:
For death each hour environs and surrounds.
lie that would know And care for future chances, cannot go, Unto those grounds,
But through a Churchyard which them bounds.
Things present shrink and die: but they that spend Their thoughts and sense
On future grief, do not remove it thence,
But it extend,
And draw the bottom out an end.

God chains the dog till night: wilt loose the chain,
And wake thy sorrow?
Wilt thou forestall it, and now grieve to-morrow,.
And then again
Grieve over freshly all thy pain?
Either grief will not come: or if it must, Do not forecast:
And while it cometh, it is almost past.
Away distrust:
My God hath promised; he is just.

PRAISE.

KlNa of glory, King of peace,
I will love thcc:
And that love may never cease,
I will move thee.
Thou hast granted my request,
Thou hast hoard me:
Thou didst note my working breast,
Thou hast spared me.
Wherefore with my utmost art
I will sing thee, And the cream of all my heart
I will bring thee.
Though my sins against me cried,
Thou didst clear me;

And alone, when they replied,
Thou didst hear me.
 Seven whole davs, not one in seven,
I will praise thee.
 In my heart, though not in heaven,
I can raise thec.
 Thou grew'st soft and moist with
tears, Thou rclentcdst.
And when Justice call'd for fears,
 Thou dissentedst.
 Small it is, in this poor sort
To enrol thce:
 Kven eternity is too short
To extol thee.

AN OFFERING.

 Come, bring thy gift. If blessings
were as slow
As men's returns, what would become
of fools?
What hast thou there? a heart / but is it
pure 1
Search well and see; for hearts have
many holes.
Yet one pure heart is nothing to bestow:
In Christ two natures met to be thy cure.
0 that within us hearts had propagation,
 Since many gifts do challenge many
hearts!
 Yet one, if good, may title to a num-
ber;
 And single things grow fruitful by
deserts.
 In public judgments one may be a na-
tion,
 And fence a plague, while others
sleep and slumber.
 Puit all I fear is, lest thy heart dis-
please,
As neither good, nor one: so oft divi-
sions
Thy lusts have made, and not thy lusts
alone;
Thy passions also have their set parti-
tions.
These parcel out thy heart: recover
these,
And thou may'st oiler many gifts in
one.
 There is a balsam, or indeed a blood.
Dropping from heaven, which doth both
cleanse and close
All sorts of wounds; of such strange
force it is.
Seek out this All-heal, and seek uo repose,

 Until thou find, and use it to thy
good:
 Then bring thy gift; and let thy hymn
be this:
 Since my sadness Into gladness,
Lord, thou dost convert,
0 accept What thou hast kept,
As thy due desert.
 Had I many, Had I any
(For this heart is none),
 All were thine
 And none of mine, -
 Surely thine alone.
 Yet thy favour May give savour
To this poor oblation;
 And it raise To be thy praise,
And be my salvation.

LONGING.

With sick and famish'd eyes,
With doubling knees and weary bones,
To thee my cries,
To thee my groans,
To thec my sighs, my tears ascend:
No end?
 My throat, my soul is hoarse;
 My heart is wither'd like a ground
 Which thou dost curse.
 My thoughts turn round,
 And make me giddy: Lord, I fall,
 Yet call.
 From thee all pity flows. Mothers arc
kind, because thou art, And dost dispose
To thorn a part: Their infants, them; and
they suck thee
 More free.
Bowels of pity, hear!
Lord of my soul, love of my mind,
how down thine car!
Let not the wind
Scatter my words, and in the same
Thy name!
 Look on my sorrows round! Mark
well my furnace! 0 what flames, What
heats abound! What griefs, what
shames! Consider, Lord; Lord, bow
thine car,
 And hear!
 Lord Jesu, thou didst bow Thy dying
head upon the tree: 0 be not now More
dead to me! Lord, hear! *Shall he that
made the ear Not tear?* Behold, thy dust
doth stir;
It moves, it creeps, it aims at thco:
Wilt thou defer
To succour me,

Thy pilo of dust, wherein each crumb
 Says, Come /
 To thee help appertains. Hast thou
left all things to their courso, And laid
the reins Upon the horse? Is all lock'd /
hath a sinner's plea
 No key?
 Indeed the world's thy book, Where
all things have their leaf assign'd Yet a
meek look I lath interlined. Thy board is
full, yet humble guests
 Find nests.
Thou tarriest, while I die,
And fall to nothing: thou dost reign,
And rule on high,
While I remain
In bitter grief: yet am I styled
Thy child.
 Lord, didst thou leave thy throne, Not
to relieve / how can it be, That thou art
grown Thus hard to me? Were sin alive,
good cause there were
 To bear.
 But now both Sin is dead, And all thy
promises live and bide. That wants his
head; These speak and chide, And in thy
bosom pour my tears,
 As theirs.
liord Je.su, hear my heart,
Which hath been broken now so long,
That every part
Hath got a tongue!
Thy beggars grow; rid them away
To-day.
My love, my sweetness, hear!
By these thy feet, at which my heart
Lies all the year,
Pluck out thy dart,
And heal my troubled breast which
cries,
Which dies.

THE BAG.

Away despair; my gracious Lord doth
hear,
Though winds and waves assault my
keel,
He doth preserve it: he doth steer,
Even when the boat seems most to reel.
Storms arc the triumph of his art:
 Well may he close his eyes, but not
his heart.
 Hast thou riot heard, that my Lord Jesus died .. "j, Then let me tell thee a
strange story.. The God of power, as he
did ride

In his majestic robes of glory, *f*— Resolved to light; and so one day

Ho did descend, undressing all the way.

The stars his tire of light and rings obtain'd,
The cloud his bow, the fire his spear,
The sky his azure mantle gain'd.
And when they ask'd, what he would wear;
He smiled, and said as he did go,

He had new clothes a making here below.

o

When he was come, as travellers arc wont,

He did repair unto an inn.

Both then, and after, many a brunt

He did endure to cancel sin: And having given the rest before,

Here he gave up his life to pay our score.

But as ho was returning, there came one
That ran upon him with a spear.
He, who came hither all alone,
Bringing nor man, nor arms, nor fear,
Received the blow upon his side, '

And straight he turn'd, and to his brethren cried,

If yc have any thing to send or write
(I have no bag, but hero is room)
Unto my Father's hands and sight,
(Believe me) it shall safely come.
That I shall mind, what you impart;

Look, you may put it very near my heart.

Or if hereafter any of my friends

Will use me in this kind, the door
Shall still be open; what he sends
I will present, and somewhat more,
Not to his hurt. Sighs will convey
Anything to me. Hark despair, away.

THE JEWS.

Poor nation, whose sweet sap and juice Our scions have purloin'd, and left you dry: "Whose streams we got by the Apostles' sluice, And use in baptism, while ye pine and die: Who by not keeping once, became a debtor;

And now by keeping lose the letter: 0 that my prayers! mine, alas! 0 that some Angel might a trumpet sound: At which the Church falling upon her face Should cry so loud, until the trump were

drown'd, And by that cry of her dear Lord obtain,

That your sweet sap might come again!

THE COLLAR.

I Struck the board, and cried, No more;
I will abroad.
What? shall I ever sigh and pine?
My lines and life are free; free as the road,
Loose as the wind, as large as store.
Shall I be still in suit?
Have I no harvest but a thorn
To let me blood, and not restore
What I have lost with cordial fruit *l*
Sure there was wine,
Before my sighs did dry it; there was corn,
Before ray tears did drown it.
Is the year only lost to me *l*
Have I no bays to crown it?
No flowers, no garlands gay *l* all blasted?
All wasted?
Not so, my heart: but there is fruit,
And thou hast hands.
Recover all thy sigh-blown age
On double pleasures: leave thy cold dispute
Of what is *fit, and not:* forsake thy cage,
Thy rope of sands,
Which petty thoughts have made, and made to thco
Good cable, to enforce and draw,
And be thy law, While thou didst wink and wouldst not see. Away; take heed: I will abroad. Call in thy death's-head there: tic up thy fears. He that forbears To suit and serve his need, Deserves his load. But as I raved and grew more fierce and wild At every word, Methought I heard one calling, *Child:* And I replied, *My Lord.* THE GLIMPSE.

Whither away delight *l*
Thou earnest but now; wilt thou so soon depart,
And give me up to-night?
For many weeks of lingering pain and smart
But one half hour of comfort for my heart *l*
Mcthinks delight should have
More skill in music, and keep bettcr time.
Wert thou a wind or wave,

They quickly go and come with lesser crime:
Flowers look about, and die not in their prime.
Thy short abode and stay
Feeds not, but adds to the desire of meat.
Lime begg'd of old (they say)
A'neighbour spring to cool his inward heat;
Which by the spring's access grew much more great.
In hope of thee my heart
Pick'd here and there a crumb, and would not die;
But constant to his part,
When as my fears foretold this, did reply,
A slender thread a gentle guest will tie.
Yet if the heart that wept
Must let thee go, return when it doth knock.
Although thy heap be kept
For future times, the droppings of the stock
May oft break forth, and never break the lock.
If I have more to spin,
The wheel shall go, so that thy stay be short.
Thou know'st how grief and sin
Disturb the work. 0 make me not their sport,
Who by thy coming may be made a Court!

ASSURANCE.

0 Spiteful bitter thought! Bitterly spiteful thought! Couldst thou invent So high a torture? Is such poison bought? Doubtless, but in the way of punishment,

When wit contrives to meet with thee,

No such rank poison can there be.

Thou saidst but even now, That all was not so fair, as I conceived, Betwixt my God and me; that I allow And coin large hopes; but, that I was deceived:

Either the league was broke, or near it;

And, that I had great cause to fear it.

And what to this *l* what more Could poison, if it had a tongue, express? What is thy aim *l* wouldst thou unlock the door To cold despairs, and gnawing pensiveness?

Wouldst thou raise devils I see, I know,

I writ thy purpose long ago.

But I will to my Father, Who heard thee say it. 0 most gracious Lord, If all the hope and comfort that I gather, Were from myself, I had not half a word,

Not half a letter to oppose

What is objected by my foes.

But thou art my desert:

And in this League, which now my foes invade,

Thou art not only to perforin thy part,

But also mine; as when the league was made,

Thou didst at once thyself indite,

And hold my hand, while I did write.

Wherefore if thou canst fail,

Then can thy truth and I: but while rocks stand,

And rivers stir, thou canst not shrink or quail:

Yea, when both rocks and all things shall disband,

Then shalt thou be my rock and tower,

And make their ruin praise thy power.

Now foolish thought go on,

Spin out thy thread, and make thereof a coat

To hide thy shame: for thou hast cast a bone,

Which bounds on thee, and will not down thy throat.

What for itself love once began,

Now love and truth will end in man.

THE CALL.

Come, my Way, my Truth, my Life:

Such a Way, as gives us breath:

Such a Truth, as ends all strife:

Such a Life, as killeth death.

Come, my Light, my Feast, my Strength

Such a Light, as shows a feast:

Such a Feast, as mends in length:

Such a Strength, as makes his guest.

Come, my Joy, my Love, my Heart:

Such a Joy, as none can move:

Such a Love, as none can part:

Such a Heart, as joys in love.

CLASPING OF HANDS.

Lord, thou art mine, and I am thine,

If mine I am: and thine much more,

Than I or ought, or can be mine.

Yet to be thine, doth me restore;

So that again I now am mine,

And with advantage mine the more.

Since this being mine, brings with it thine,

And thou with me dost thee restore.

If I without thee would be mine,

I neither should be mine nor thine.

Lord, I am thine, and thou art mine:

So mine thou art, that something more

I may presume thee mine, than thine.

For thou didst suffer to restore

Not thee, but me, and to be mine:

And with advantage mine the more,

Since thou in death wast none of thine,

Yet then sis mine didst me restore.

0 be mine still! still make me thine;

Or rather make no Thine and Mine!

PRAISE.

Lord, I will mean and speak thy praise,

Thy praise alone.

My busy heart shall spin it all my days:

And when it stops for want of store,

Then will I wring it with a sigh or groan,

That thou may'st yet have more.

When thou dost favour any action,

It runs, it flies:

All things concur to give it a perfection.

That which had but two legs before,

When thou dost bless, hath twelve: one wheel doth rise

To twenty then, or more.

But when thou dost on business blow,

It hangs, it clogs:

Not all the teams of Albion in a row

Can hale or draw it out of door.

Legs are but stumps, and Pharaoh's wheels but logs,

And struggling hinders more.

Thousands of things do thee employ

In ruling all

This spacious Globe: Angels must have their joy,

Devils their rod, the sea his shore,

The winds their stint: and yet when I did call,

Thou hcardst my call, and more.

I have not lost one single tear: But when mine eyes

Did weep to heaven, they found a bottle there

(As we have boxes for the poor)

Ready to take them in; yet of a size

That would contain much more.

But after thou hadst slipt a drop

From thy right eye (Which there did hang like streamers near the top

Of some fair Church, to show the sore And bloody battle which thou once didst try),

The glass was full, and more.-

Wherefore I sing. Yet since my heart,

Though press'd, runs thin; 0 that I might some other hearts convert,

And so take up at use good store:

That to thy chests there might be coming in

Both all my praise, and more!

JOSEPH'S COAT. Wounded I sing, tormented I indite,

Thrown down I fall into a bed, and rest:

Sorrow hath changed its note: such is His will

Who changcth all things, as him pleascth best.

For well he knows, if but one grief and smart

Among my many had his full career,

Sure it would carry with it even my heart,

And both would run until they found a bier

To fetch the body; both being due to grief.

But he hath spoil'd the race; and given to anguish

One of Joy's coats, 'ticing it with relief

To linger in me, and together languish.

I live to show his power, who once did bring

My *joys to weep,* and now *my griefs to sing.*

THE PULLEY.

When God at first made man, Having a glass of blessings standing by; Let us (said he) pour on him all we can: Let the world's riches, which dispersed lie,

Contract into a span.

So strength first made a way; Then beauty flow'd, then wisdom, honour, pleasure When almost all was out, God made a stay, Perceiving that alone, of all his treasure,

Rest in the bottom lay.

For if I should (said he)

Bestow this jewel also on my creature,

He would adore my gifts instead of me,

And rest in Nature, not the God of Nature:

So both should losers be.

Yet let him keep the rest,
But keep them with repining restless-
ness:
Let him be rich and weary, that at least,
If goodness lead him not, yet weariness
May toss him to my breast.

THE PRIESTHOOD.

Blest Order, which in power dost so excel,
That with the one hand thou liftest to the
sky,
And with the other throwest down to
hell,
In thy just censures; fain would I draw
nigh;
Fain put thee on, exchanging my lay-
sword
For that of the holy Word.

But thou art fire, sacred and hallow'd
fire;
And I but earth and clay: should I pre-
sume
To wear thy habit, the severe attire
My slender compositions might con-
sume.
I am both foul and brittle, much unfit
To deal in holy Writ.

Yet have I oftcu seen, by cunning
hand
And force of fire, what curious things
arc made
Of wretched earth. Where once I
scorn'd to stand,
That earth is fitted by the fire and trade
Of skilful Artists, for the boards of
those
Who make the bravest shows.

But since those great ones, bo they
ne'er so great,
Come from the earth, from whence
those vessels come;
So that at once both feeder, dish, and
meat,
Have one beginning and one final sum:
I do not greatly wonder at the sight,
If earth in earth delight.

But the holy men of God such vessels
are,
As serve him up, who all the world
commands.
When God vouchsafcth to become our
fare,
Their hands convey him, who conveys
their hands:
0 what pure things, most pure must
those things be,
Who bring my God to me!

Wherefore I dare not, I, put forth my
hand
To hold the Ark, although it seem to
shake
Through th' old sins and new doctrines
of our land.
Only, since God doth often vessels
make
Of lowly matter for high uses meet,
I throw me at his feet.

There will I lie, until my Maker seek
For some mean stuiF whereon to show
his skill:
Then is my time. The distance of the
meek
Doth flatter power. Lest good come
short of ill
In praising might, the poor do by sub-
mission
What pride by opposition.

THE SEARCH.

WIllTHEK, 0, whither art thou (led,
My Lord, my love?
My searches arc my daily bread;
Yet never prove.

My knees pierce th' earth, mine eyes
the sky And yet the sphere
And centre both to me deny
That thou art there.

Yet can I mark how herbs below
Grow green and gay;
As if to meet thee they did know,
While I decay.

Yet can I mark how stars above
Simper and shine,
As having keys unto thy love,
While poor I pino.

I sent a sigh to seek thee out,
Deep drawn in pain,
Wing'd like an arrow: but my scout
Returns in vain.

I turn'd another (having store)
Into a groan,
Because the search was dumb before:
But all was one.

Lord, dost thou some new fabric
mould
Which favour wins,
And keeps thee present, leaving th'
old Unto their sins?

Where is my God / what hidden
place
Conceals thec still?

What covert dare eclipse thy face /
Is it thy will /

0 let not that of any thing:
Let rather brass,
Or steel, or mountains be thy ring,
And I will pass.

Thy will such an intrenching is,
As passcth thought:
To it all strength, all subtilties
Are things of nought.

Thy will such a strange distance is,
As that to it
East and West touch, the poles do kiss,
And parallels meet.

Since then my grief must be as large
As is thy space, Thy distance from
me; see my charge,
Lord, see my case.

0 take these bars, these lengths, away;
Turn, and restore mc: Be not
Almighty, let me say, *Against,* but *for*
me.

When thou dost turn, and wilt be
near: "What edge so keen,
What point so piercing can appear
To come between

For as thy absence doth excel
All distance known:
So doth thy nearness bear the bell,
Making two one.

GRIEF. 0 Who will give me tears? Come,
all ye springs,
Dwell in my head and eyes: come,
clouds, and raiu
My grief hath need of all the watery
things,
That Nature hath produced. Let every
vein
Suck up a river to supply mine eyes,
My weary weeping eyes too dry for me,
Unless they get new conduits, new sup-
plies,
To bear them out, and with my state
agree.
What arc two shallow fords, two little
spouts
Of a less world? the greater is but.small,
A narrow cupboard for my griefs and
doubts,
Which want provision in the midst of
all.
Verses, yc arc too fine a thing, too wise
For my rough sorrows: cease, be dumb
and mute,
Give up your feet and running to mine

eyes,
And keep your measures for some
lover's lute,
Whose grief allows him music and a
rhyme:
For mine excludes both measure, tune,
and time.
Alas, my God!
To make me sigh, and seek, and faint,
and die,
Until I had some place, where I might
sing,
And serve thee; and not only I,
But all my wealth, and family might
combine
To set thy honour up, as our design?
And thou when after much delay,
Much wrestling, many a combat, this
dear end,
So much desired, is given, to take away
My power to serve thee: to unbend
All my abilities, my designs confound,
And lay my threatenings bleeding on
the ground.
One ague dwelleth in my bones.
Another in my soul (the memory
What I would do for thee, if once my
groans
Could be allow'd for harmony);
I am in all a weak disabled thing,
Save in the sight thereof, where strength
doth sting.
Besides, things sort not to my will,
Even when my will doth study thy
renown:
Thou turn'st the edge of all things on
me still,
Taking me up to throw me down:
So that, even when my hopes seem to be
sped,
I am to grief alive, to them as/dead.
To have my aim, and yet to be - "/./-,
Farther from it than when I bent my
bqw_:
To make my hopes my torture, and the
fee
Of all my woes another woe,
Is in the midst of delicates to need,
And even in Paradise to be a weed.
-_ Ah, my dear Father, ease my smart!
These contrarieties crush me: these
cross actions
Do wind a rope about, and cut my heart:
And yet since these thy contradictions
Are properly a Cross felt by thy Son,

With but four words, my words, *Thy
will be done.*

THE FLOWER.

How fresh, 0 Lord, how sweet and
clean Are thy returns! even as the flowers in spring; To which, besides their
own demean,
The late-past frosts tributes of pleasure
bring.
Grief melts away
Like snow in May,
As if there were no such cold thing.
Who would luive thought my shriv-
ell'd heart Could have recover'd green-
ness? It was gone
Quito under ground; as flowers de-
part To see their Mother-root, when
they have blown; Where they together
All the hard weather, Dead to the world,
keep house unknown.
These are thy wonders, Lord of power,
Killing and quickening, bringing down
to hell
And up to heaven in an hour;
Making a chiming of a passing bell.
We say amiss,
This or that is:
Thy Word is nil, if we could spell.
0 that I once past changing were, Fast in
thy Paradise, where no flower can with-
er!
Many a spring I shoot up fair, Offering
at heaven, growing and groaning thith-
er: Nor doth my flower Want a spring-
shower, My sins and I joining together.
But while I grow in a straight lino,
Still upwards bent, as if heaven were
mine own,
Thy anger comes, and I decline:
What frost to that? what pole is not the
zone
Where all tilings burn,
When thou dost turn,
And the least frown of thine is shown?
And now in age bud again,
After so many deaths I live and write;
I once more smell the dew and rain,
And relish versing: 0 my only light,
It cannot be
That I am he,
On whom thy tempests fell at night.
These are thy wonders, Lord of love.
To make us see we are but (lowers that
glide:
Which when we once can find and

prove,
Thou hast a garden for us, where to
bide.
Who Mould bo more,
Swelling through store,
DO
Forfeit their Paradise by their pride.

DOTAGE.

False glozing pleasures, casks of happi-
ness,
Foolish night-fires, women's and chil-
dren's wishes,
Chases in arras, gilded emptiness,
Shadows well mounted, dreams in a ca-
reer,
Embroider'd lies, nothing between two
dishes;
These are the pleasures here.
True earnest sorrows, rooted mis-
eries,
Anguish in grain, vexations ripe and
blown,
Sure-footed griefs, solid calamities,
Plain demonstrations, evident and clear,
Fetching their proofs even from the very
bono;
These are the sorrows here.
But oh the folly of distracted men,
Who griefs in earnest, joys in jest pur-
sue;
Preferring, like brute beasts, a loath-
some den
Before a court, even that above so clear,
Where are no sorrows, but delights
more true
Than miseries are here!

THE SON.

Let foreign nations of their language
boast,
What fine variety each tongue affords:
I like our language, as our men and
coast;
Who cannot dress it well, want wit, not
words.
Now neatly do we give one only name
To Parent's issue and the Sun's bright
star!
A Son is light and fruit; a fruitful flame
Chasing the Father's dimness, carried
far
From the first man in the East, to fresh
and new
Western discoveries of posterity.
So in one word our Lord's humility
Wo turn upon him in a sense most true:

For what Christ once in humbleness be-
gan,
We him in glory call, *The Son of Man.*
A TRUE HYMN.
My joy, my life, my crown!
My heart was meaning:ill the day,
Somewhat it fain would say:
And still it runneth muttering up and
down
With only this, *My joy, my life, my
crown!*
Yet slight not these few words;
If truly said, they may take part
Among the best in art.
The fineness which a Hymn or Psalm
affords,
Is, when the soul unto the lines accords.
He who craves all the mind.
And all the soul, and strength, and time,
If the words only rhyme,
Justly complains, that somewhat is be-
hind
To make his Verse, or write a Hymn in
kind.
Whereas if the heart be moved.
Although the Verse be somewhat scant,
God doth supply the want.
As when the heart says (sighing to be
approved).
Oh, could I love! and stops; (jod writcth,
Loved.
THE ANSWER.
My comforts drop and melt away like
snow:
I shake my head, and all the thoughts
and ends,
Which my fierce youth did bandy, fall
and flow
Like leaves about me, or like summer
friends,
        M
Flies of estates and sunshine. But to
all,
Who think me eager, hot, and under-
taking,
But in my prosecutions slack and
small;
As a young exhalation, newly wak-
ing,
Scorns his first bed of dirt, and means
the sky;
But cooling by the way, grows pursy
and slow,
And settling to a cloud, doth live and
die

In that dark state of tears: to all, that
so
Show me, and set me, I have one re-
ply,
Which they that know the rest, know
more than I.
A DIALOGUE-ANTIIEM.
CHRISTIAN, DEATH.
Car. Alas, poor Death! where is thy glo-
ry *l*
Where is thy famous force, thy an-
cient sting?
Dea. *Alas! poor mortal, void of story,
Go spell and read hoiu I have kill'd thy
King.*
Chr. Poor Death! and who was hurt
thereby *l*
Thy curso being laid on him makes
thee accurst.
Dea. *Let losers talk, yet thou shall
die;
These arms shall crush thee.*
Chr. Sparc not, do thy worst.
I shall bo ono day better than before:
Thou so much worse, that thou shall be
no more.
THE WATElt-COURSE.
Thou who dost dwell and linger here
below,
Since the condition of this world is frail,
Where of all plants afllictions soonest
grow;
If troubles overtake thee, do not wail:
For who cau look for less that loveth-
c ..,.
(Strife?
But rather turn the pipe, and water's
course
To serve thy sins, and furnish thee
with store
Of sovereign tears, springing from
true remorse:
That so in pureness thou may'st him
adore wi *i i /,* (Salvation.
Who gives to man, as lie sees fit, _
Damnation.
SELF-CONDEMNATION. Thou who con-
demncst Jewish hate,
For choosing *Barabbas* a murderer
Before the Lord of glory;
Look back upon thine own estate,
Call home thine eye (that busy wander-
er),
That choice may be thy story.
lie that doth love, and love amiss, This

world's delights before true Christian
joy, Hath made a Jewish choice: The
world an ancient murderer is; Thou-
sands of souls it hath and doth destroy
With her enchanting voice. He that hath
made a sorry wedding
Between his soul and gold, and hath
preferr'd
False gain before the true,
Hath done what he condemns in read-
ing:
For he hath sold for money his dear
Lord,
And is a Judas-Jew.
Thus we prevent the last great day,
And judgo ourselves. That light which
sin and passion
Did before dim and choke,
When once those snuffs are ta'en away,
Shines bright and clear, even unto con-
demnation,
Without excuse or cloak.
BITTER-SWEET.
Ah, my dear angry Lord,
Since thou dost love, yet strike j
Cast down, yet help afford:
Sure I will do the like.
I will complain, yet praise;
I will bewail, approve:
And all my sour-sweet days
I will lament, and love.
THE GLANCE.
f When first thy sweet and gracious eye
Vouchsafed even in the midst of youth
and night To look upon me, who before
did lie
Weltering in sin
I felt a sugar'd strange delight, Pass-
ing all Cordials made by any Art,
Bedew, embalm, and overrun my heart,
And take it in.
Since that time many a bitter storm
My soul hath felt, even able to destroy,
Had the malicious and ill-meaning harm
His swing and sway: But still thy sweet
original joy, Sprung from thine eye, did
work within my soul, And surging
griefs, when they grew bold, control,
And got the day.
If thy first glance so powerful be, A
mirth but open'd and scal'd up again;
What wonders shall we feel, when we
shall see Thy full-eyed love! When thou
shalt look us out of pain, And one aspect
of thine spend in delight More than a

thousand suns disburse in light, In Heaven above.

THE TWENTY-THIRD PSALM.

The God of love my shepherd is.
And he that doth me feed:
While he is mine, and I am his,
What can I want or need *l*

He leads me to the tender grass,
Where I both feed and rest;
Then to the streams that gently pass
' In both I have the best.

Or if I stray, ho doth convert,
And bring my mind in framo:
And all this not for my desert,
But for his holy name.

Yea, in death's shady, black abode
Well may I walk, not fear:
For thou art with me, and thy rod
To guide, thy staff to bear.

Nay, thou dost make me sit and dine,
Even in my enemies' sight;
My head with oil, my cup with wine
Runs over day and night.

Surely thy sweet and wondrous love
Shall measuro all my days;
And as it never shall remove,
So neither shall my praise.

MARY MAGDALEN.

When blessed *Mary* wiped her Saviour's feet
(Whose precepts she had trampled on before),
And wore them for a Jewel on her head,
Showing his steps should be tho street,
Wherein she thenceforth evermore
With pensive humbleness would live and tread:

Sho bciug stain'd herself, why did she strive
To make him clean, who could not bo defiled?

Why kept she not her tears for her own faults,
And not his feet *l* Though we could dive
In tears like Seas, our sins arc piled

Deeper than they, in words, and works, and thoughts.

Dear soul, she knew who did vouchsafe and deign
To bear her filth: and that her sins did dash
Even God himself: wherefore she was not loath,

As she had brought wherewith to stain,

So to bring in wherewith to wash:
And yet in washing one, she washed both.

AARON. Iiouni;s3 on the head,
Light and perfections on the breast,
Harmonious bells below, raising the dead
To lead them unto life and rest.
Thus arc true *A irons* drcst.

Profaneness in my head,
Defects and darkness in my breast,
A noise of passions ringing mc for dead
Unto a place where is no rest:
Poor Priest thus am I drest.

Only another head
I have, another heart and breast,
Another music, making live, not dead,
Without whom I could have no rest:
In him I am well drcst.

Christ is my only head,
My alone only heart and breast,
My only music, striking me even dead;
That to the old man I may rest,
And be in him new drest.

So holy in my head, Perfect and light in my dear breast, My doctrine tuned by Christ (who is not dead, But lives in me while I do rest),

Come, people; *Aaron's* drest.

THE ODOUR.
2 Cor. ii.

How sweetly doth *My Master* sound!
My Master!

As ambergis leaves a rich scent
Unto the taster:
So do these words a sweet content,
An Oriental fragrancy, *My Master.*

With these all day I do perfume my mind,
My mind even thrust into them both;
That I might find
What Cordials make this curious broth,
This broth of smells, that feeds and fats my mind.

My Master, shall I speak *l* 0 that to thee
My Servant were a little so,
As flesh may be;
That these two words might creep and grow
To some degree of spiciness to thec!

Then should the Pomander, which was before
A speaking sweet, mend by reflection,
And tell me more:

For pardon of my imperfection
Would warm and work it sweeter than before.

For when *My Master,* which alone is sweet,
And even in my unworthincss pleasing,
Shall call and meet,
My Servant, as thee not displeasing,
That call is but the breathing of the sweet.

This breathing would with gains by sweetening me
(As sweet things traffic when they meet)
Return to thee.
And so this new commerce and sweet
Should all my life employ, and busy me.

THE FOIL. If we could sec below
The sphere of virtue, and each shining grace,
As plainly as that above doth show;
This were the better sky, the brighter place.
God hath made stars the foil
To set off virtues: griefs to set off sinning:
Yet in this wretched world we toil.
As if grief were not foul, nor virtue winning.

THE FORERUNNERS.

The Harbingers arc come. See, see their mark;
White is their colour, and behold my head.
But must they have my brain? must they dispark
Those sparkling notions, which therein were bred *l*
Must dulness turn me to a clod *l*
Yet have they left me, *Thou art still my God.*

Good men ye be, to leave me my best room,
Even all my heart, and what is lodged there:
I pass not, I, what of the rest become,
So, *Thou art still my God,* be out of fear.
He will be pleased with that ditty;
And if I please him, I write fine and witty.

Farewell sweet phrases, lovely metaphors:
But will ye leave me thus? when ye before

Of stews and brothels only knew the doors,
Then did I wash you with my tears, and more,
Brought you to Church well drest and clad:
My God must have my best, even all I had.

Lovely enchanting language, sugarcane,
Honey of roses, whither wilt thou fly?
Hath some fond lover 'ticcd thee to thy bane?
And wilt thou leavo the Church, and love a sty?
Fie, thou wilt soil thy broider'd coat,
And hurt thyself, and him that sings the note.
Let foolish lovers, if they will love dung,
With Canvas, not with Arras, clothe their shame:
Let Folly speak in her own native tongue.
True beauty dwells on high: ours is a flame

But borrow'd thence to light us thither. Beauty and beauteous words should go together.

Yet if you go, I pass not; take your way:
For, *Thou art still my God,* is all that ye
Perhaps with more embellishment can say.
Go, birds of spring: let winter have his fee;
Let a bleak paleness chalk the door,
So all within be livelier than before.

THE ROSE.

Press me not to take more pleasure
In this world of sugar'd lies,
And to use a larger measure
Than my strict, yet welcome size.
First, there is no pleasure here:
Colour'd griefs indeed there are,
Blushing woes, that look as clear,
As if they could beauty spare.
Or if such deceits there be,
Such delights I mean to say;
There are no such things to me,
Who have pass'd my right away.
But I will not much oppose
Unto what you now advise:
Only take this gentle Rose,
And therein my answer lies.

What is fairer than a rose?
What is sweeter'(yet it purgeth.
Purgings enmity disclose,
Enmity forbearance urgeth.
If then all that worldlings prize
Be contracted to a rose;
Sweetly there indeed it lies,
But it bitcth in the close.
So this flower doth judge and sentence
Worldly joys to be a scourge:
For they all produce repentance,
And repentance is a purge.
But I health, not physic choose:
Only though I you oppose,
Say that fairly I refuse,
For my answer is a rose..

DISCIPLINE.

Throw away thy rod.
Throw away thy wrath:
0 my God,
Take the gentle path.
For my heart's desire
Unto thine is bent:
I aspire
To a full consent.
Not a word or look
I affect to own,
But by book,
And thy book alone.
Though 1 fail, I weep:
Though I halt in pace,
Yet I creep
To the throne of grace.
Then let wrath remove;
Love will do the deed:
For with love
Stony hearts will bleed.
Love is swift of foot;
Love's a man of war,
And can shoot,
And can hit from far.
Who can 'scape his bow?
That which wrought on thee,
Brought thee low,
Needs must work on inc.
Throw away thy rod;
Thoudi man frailties hath,
o Thou art God:
Throw away thy wrath.

THE INVITATION.

Come yc hither all, whoso taste
Is your waste; Save your cost, and
mend your fare. God is here prepared
and dress'd,

And the feast, God, in whom all dainties are.
Come yc hither all, whom wine Doth define,
Naming you not to your good:
Weep what yc have drunk amiss,
And drink this,
Which before ye drink is blood.
. Come yc hither all, whom pain Doth arraign,
Bringing all your sins to sight:
Taste and fear not: God is here
In this cheer,
And on sin doth cast the fright.
Como ye hither all, whom joy Doth destroy,
While yc graze without your bounds:
Here is joy that drowncth quite
Your delight,
As a flood the lower grounds.
Conic ye hither all, whose love
Is your dove, And exalts you to the sky: Here is love, which, having brcath
Even in death, After death can never die.
Lord, I have invited all,
And I shall Still invite, still call to thee: For it seems but just and right
In my sight, Where is all, there all should be.

TUB BANQUET.

Welcome sweet and sacred cheer, Welcome dear;
With me, in me, live and dwell:
For thy neatness passcth sight,
Thy delight
Passcth tongue to taste or tell.
0 what sweetness from the bowl Fills my soul,
Such as is, and makes divine!
Is some star (fled from the sphere) Melted there,
As wc sugar melt in wine?
Or liath sweetness in the bread Made ii head
To subdue the smell of sin,
Flowers, and gums, and powders giving All their living,
Lest the enemy should win *l*
Doubtless, neither star nor flower I lath the power
Such a sweetness to impart:
Oidy God, who gives perfumes, Flesh assumes,
And with it perfumes my heart.

But as Pomanders and wood
Still arc good,
   Yet being bruised arc better scented;
   God, to show how far his love
Could improve;
   Here, as broken, is presented.
   When I had forgot my birth,
And on earth
   In delights of earth was drown'd;
   God took blood, and needs would be
Spilt with mo,
   And so found me on the ground.
   Having raised me to look up,
   In a cup Sweetly he doth meet my
taste. But I still being low and short,
   Far from court, Wine becomes a wing
at last.
   For with it alone I fly To the sky:
Where I wipe mine eyes, and see
What I seek, for what I sue;
Him I view,
Who hath done so much for me.
   Let the wonder of this pity Be my dit-
ty,
And take up my lines and life:
Hearken under pain of death,
Hands and breath,
Strive in this, and love the strife.

THE POSY.

Let wits contest,
And with their words and posies win-
dows fill
Less than the least
Of all thy mercies, is my posy still.
This on my ring,
This by my picture, in my book I write;
Whether I sing,
Or say, or dictate, this is my delight.
Invention rest;
Comparisons go play; wit use thy will:
Less than t/ie least
Of all God's mercies, is my posy still.
N

A PARODY.

Soul's joy, when thou art gone,
   And I alone,
"Which cannot be, Because thou dost
abide in me, And I depend on thee;
   Yet when thou dost suppress
   The cheerfulness Of thy abode,
And in my powers not stir abroad,
But leave me to my load:
0 what a damp and shade
Doth me invade!
No stormy night

Can so afflict or so affright
As thy eclipsed light.
   Ah, Lord! do not withdraw.
   Lest want of awe
   Make sin appear; And when thou dost
but shine less clear, Say, that thou art
not here.
   And then what life I have,
   While Sin doth rave, And falsely
boast,
That I may seek, but thou art lost!
Thou and alone thou know'st.
0 what a deadly cold
   Doth me infold! I half believe, That
Sin says true: but while I grieve, Thou
comest and dost relieve.

,v.ijm Jn A'j-«a-vvvc5 THE ELIXIR.

Teach me, my God and King,
In all things thee to see,
And what I do in any thing,
To do it as for thee:

Not rudely, as a beast,
To run into an action;
But still to make thee prcpossest,
And give it his perfection.

A man that looks on glass,
On it may stay his eye;
Or if he pleascth, through it pass,
And then the heaven espy.

All may of thee partake:
Nothing can be so mean,
Which with his tincture (for thy sake)
Will not grow bright and clean.

A servant with this clause
Makes drudgery divine:
Who sweeps a room, as for thy laws,
Makes that and th' action fine.

This is the famous stono
That tumcth all to gold:
For that which God doth touch and own
Cannot for less be told.

A WREATH.

   A Wreathed garland of deserved
praise,
   Of praise deserved, unto thee I give,
   I give to thee, who knowest all my
ways,
   My crooked winding ways, wherein I
live,
   Wherein I die, not live; for life is
straight,
   Straight as a line, and ever tends to
thee,
   To thee, who art more far above deceit,

Than deceit seems above simplicity.
   Give mc simplicity, that I may live,
   So live and like, that I may know thy
ways,
   Know them and practise them: then
shall I give
   For this poor wreath, give thco a
crown of praise.

DEATH.

Death, thou wast once an uncouth
hideous thing,
Nothing but bones,
The sad efTcct of sadder groans:
Thy mouth was open, but thou couldst
not sing.

   For we considcr'd thee as at some six
Or ten years hence,
After the loss of life and sense,
Flesh being turn'd to dust, and bones to
sticks.

Wc look'd on tins side of thee,, shooting
short;
Where wc did find
The shells of (ledge souls left behind,
Dry dust, which sheds no tears, but may
extort.

   But since our Saviour's death did put
some blood
Into thy face:
Thou art grown fair and full of grace.
Much in request, much sought for, as a
good.

   For wc do now behold thee gay and
glad,
As at doomsday;
When souls shall wear their new array,
And all thy bones with beauty shall be
clad.

   Therefore wc can go die as sleep, and
trust
Half that wo have
Unto an honest faithful grave;
Making our pillows cither down, or
dust.

DOOMSDAY.

Come away,
Make no delay.
Summon all the dust to rise,
Till it stir, and rub the eyes;
While this member jogs the other,
Each one whispering, Live you, brother
f

Come away,
Make this the day.
Dust, alas! no music feels,

But thy trumpet: then it kneels,
As peculiar notes and strains
Cure Tarantula's raging pains.
Come away,
0 make no stay!
Let the graves make their confession,
Lest at length they plead possession:
Flesh's stubbornness may have
Read that lesson to the grave.
Come away,
Thy flock doth stray.
Some to the winds their body lend,
And in them many drown a friend:
Some in noisome vapours grow
To a plague and public woe.
Come away,
Help our decay.
Man is out of order hurl'd,
Parcell'd out to all the world.
Lord, thy broken consort raise,
And the music shall bo praise.

JUDGMENT.

Almighty Judge, how shall poor wretches brook
Thy dreadful look, Able a heart of iron to appal,
When thou shalt call For every man's peculiar book? What others mean to do, I know not well;
Yet I hear tell, That some will turn thee to some leaves therein So void of sin, That they in merit shall excel.
But I resolve, when thou shalt call for mine, That to decline,
And thrust a Testament into thy hand:
Let that be scann'd.
There thou shalt find my faults arc thine.

HEAVEN.

0 Who will show me those delights on high?
Echo. J.
Thou Echo, thou art mortal, all men know.
Echo. No.
Wert thou not born among the trees and leaves?
Echo. Leaves.
And are there any leaves, that still abide?
Echo. Bide.
What leaves arc they? impart the matter wholly.
Echo. llohj.
Are holy leaves the Echo then of

bliss?
Echo. Yes.
Then tell me, what is that supreme delight?
Echo. Lhjht.
Light to the mind: what shall the will enjoy?
Echo. Joy.
But arc there cares and business with the pleasure?
Echo. Leisure.
Light, joy, and leisure; but shall they perscver?
Echo. Ever. LOVE.
Love bade me weleome; yet my soul drew back, Guilty of dust and sin.
But quick-eyed Love, observing me grow slack
From my first entrance in,
Drew nearer to me, sweetly questioning,
If I lack'd any thing.
A guest, I answer'd, worthy to be here: Love said, You shall be he.
I the unkind, ungrateful? Ah, my dear, I cannot look on thee.
Love took my hand, and smiling did reply,
Who made the eyes but I1
Truth, Lord, but I have marr'd them: let my shame
Go where it doth deserve. And know you not, says Love, who bore the blame?
My dear, then I will serve. You must sit down, says Love, and taste my meat:
So I did sit and eat.
FINIS. *Glory be to God on high, and on earth peace,*
good-will towards men.
THE CIIURCn MILITANT.
Almighty Lord, who from thy glorious throne
Scest and rulest all things even as one:
The smallest Ant or Atom knows thy power,
Known also to each minute of an hour:
Much more do Commonweals acknowledge thee,
And wrap their policies in thy decree,
Complying with thy counsels, doing nought
Which doth not meet with an eternal thought.
But above all, thy Church and Spouse

doth prove
Not the decrees of power, but bands of love.
Early didst thou arise to plant this Vine,
Which might the more endear it to be thine.
Spices come from the East; so did thy Spouse,
Trim as the light, sweet as the laden boughs
Of *Noah's* shady vine, chaste as the dove,
Prepared and fitted to receive thy love.
The course was westward, that the sun might light
As well our understanding as our sight.
Where th' Ark did rest, there *Abraham* began
To bring the other Ark from *Canaan.*
Moses pursued this: but King *Solomon* Finish'd and-fix'd the old religion.
When it grew loose, the Jews did hope in vain
By nailing Christ to fasten it again.
But to the Gentiles he bore cross and all,
Rending with earthquakes the partition-wall.
Only whereas the Ark in glory shone,
Now with the cross, as with a staff, alone,
Religion, like a pilgrim, westward bent,
Knocking at all doors, ever as she went.
Yet as the Sun, though forward be his flight,
Listens behind him, and allows some light,
Till all depart: so went the Church her way,
Letting, while one foot stepp'd, the other stay
Among the eastern nations for a time,
Till both removed to the western clime.
To *Egypt* first she came, where they did prove
Wonders of anger once, but now of love.
The ten Commandments there did flourish more
Than the ten bitter plagues had done before.
Holy *Macarius* and great *Anthony*
Made *Pharaoh Moses,* changing the history.
Goshen was darkness, *Egypt* full of lights,

Nilus for monsters brought forth Is-
raelites.

Such power hath mighty Baptism to
produce,

For things misshapen, things of highest use.

*How dear to me, 0 God, thy counsels
are! Who may with thee compare?*

Religion thence fled into *Greece,* where
Arts

Gave her the highest place in all
men's hearts.

Learning was posed, Philosophy was
set,

Sophistcrs taken in a Fisher's net.

Plato and *Aristotle* were at a loss,

And wheel'd about again to spell
Christ's-Cross.

Prayers chased syllogisms into their
den,

And *Ergo* was transform'd into
Amen.

Though *Greece* took horse as soon as
Egypt did,

And *Rome* as both; yet *Egypt* faster
rid,

And spent her period and prefixed
time

Before the other. *Greece* being past
her prime,

Religion went to *Rome,* subduing
those,

Who, that they might subdue, made
all their foes.

The Warrior his dear scars no more
resounds,

But seems to yield Christ hath the
greater wounds;

Wounds willingly endured to work
his blis3,

Who by an ambush lost his Paradise.

The great heart stoops, and takcth
from the dust

A sad repentance, not the spoils of
lust:

Quitting his spear, lest it should
pierce again ιTim in his members, who
for him was slain.

The Shepherd's hook grew to a Sceptre here,

Giving new names and numbers to
the year.

But th' Empire dwelt in *Greece,* to
comfort them,

Who were cut short in *Alexanders*
stem.

In both of these Prowess and Arts did
tame

And tunc men's hearts against the
Gospel came:

Which using, and not fearing skill in
the one,

Or strength in th' other, did erect her
throne,

Many a rent and struggling th' Empire knew (As dying things arc wont),
until it flew

At length to *Germain/,* still westward
bending.

And there the Church's festival attending:

That as before Empire and Arts made
way (For no less harbingers would serve
than they),

So they might still, and point us out
the place,

Where first the Church should raise
her downcast face.

Strength levels grounds, Art makes a
garden there;

Then showers Religion, and makes
all to bear.

Spain in the Empire shared with *Ger-
many,*

But *England* in the higher victory;

Giving the Church a crown to keep
her state,

And not go less than she had done of
late.

Constantino's British line meant this of
old,

And did this mystery wrap up and fold
Within a sheet of paper, which was rent
From Time's great Chronicle, and hith-
er sent.

Thus both the Church and Sun together
ran
Unto the farthest old meridian.

*How dear to me, 0 God, thy counsels
are!*

Who may with thee compare?

Much about one and the same time and
place,
Both where and when the Church began
her race,
Sin did set out of Eastern *Babylon,*
And travell'd westward also: journeying on
He chid the Church away, where'er he
came,

Breaking her peace, and tainting her
good name.
At first he got to *Egypt,* and did sow
Gardens of gods, which every year did
grow,
Fresh and fine deities. They were at
great cost,
"Who for a god clearly a sallet lost.
Ah, what a thing is man devoid of grace,
Adoring Garlic with an humble face,
Begging his food of that which he may
cat,
Starving the while he worshippcth his
meat!
Who makes a root his god, how low is
he,
If God and man be sevcr'd infinitely!
What wretchedness can give him any
room,
Whose house is foul, while he adores
his broom /
None will believe this now, though
money be
In us the same transplanted foolery.
Thus Sin in *Egypt* sneaked for a while;
His highest was an ox or crocodile,
And such poor game. Thence he to
Greece doth pass,
And being craftier much than Goodness
was,

He left behind him garrisons of sins,

To make good that which every day
he wins.

Here Sin took heart, and for a garden-
bed

Rich shrines and oracles he purchased: lie grew a gallant, and would
needs foretell

As well what should befall, as what
befell.

Nay, he became a Poet, and would
serve

His pills of sublimate in that conserve.

The world came both with hands and
purses full

To this great lottery, and all would
pull.

But all was glorious cheating, brave
deceit,

Where some poor truths were shuf-
fled for a bait

To credit him, and to discredit those,

Who after him should braver truths
disclose.

From *Greece* he went to *Rome:* and as before

He was a God, now he's an Emperor. *Nero* and others lodged him bravely there,

Put him in trust to rule the Roman sphere

Glory was his chief instrument of old: Pleasure succeeded straight, when that grew cold:

Which soon was blown to such a mighty flame,

That though our Saviour did destroy the game,

Disparking oracles, and all their treasure,

Setting affliction to encounter pleasure;

Yet did a rogue with hope of carnal joy,

Cheat the most subtle nations. Who so coy,

So trim, as *Greece* and *Egypt?* yet their hearts

Are given over, for their curious arts,

To such Mahometan stupidities,

As the old Heathen would deem prodigies.

How dear to me, O God, thy counsels are! Who may with thee compare? Only the West and *Rome* do keep them free From this contagious infidelity.

And this is all the Rock, whereof they boast,

As *Rome* will one day find unto her cost.

Sin being not able to extirpate quite The Churches here, bravely resolved one night

To be a Churchman too, and wear a Mitre:

The old debauched Ruffian would turn writer.

I saw him in his study, where he sate Busy in controversies sprung of late.

A gown and pen became him wondrous well:

His grave aspect had more of heaven than hell:

Only there was a handsome picture by,

To which he lent a corner of his eye.

As Sin in *Greece* a Prophet was before,

And in old *Rome* a mighty Emperor;

So now being Priest, he plainly did profess

To make a jest of Christ's three Offices:

The rather since his scatter'd juggliugs were

United now in one both time and sphere.

From *Egypt* he took petty deities,

From *Greece* oracular infallibilities,

And from old *Rome* the liberty of pleasure,

By free dispensings of the Church's treasure.

Then in memorial of his ancient throne,

He did surname his palace, *Babylon.*

Yet that he might the better gain all nations,

And make that name good by their transmigrations;

From all these places, but at divers times, he took fine vizards to conceal his crimes:

From *Egypt* Anchorism and retiredness,

Learning from *Greece,* from old *Rome* stateliness;

And blending these, he carried all men's eyes,

While Truth sat by, counting his victories:

Whereby he grew apace and scorn'd to use

Such force as once did captivate the Jews;

But did bewitch, and finally work each nation

Into a voluntary transmigration.

All post to *Rome:* Princes submit their necks

Either to his public foot or private tricks.

It did not fit his gravity to stir,

Nor his long journey, nor his gout and fur:

Therefore he sent out able Ministers,

Statesmen within, without doors Cloisterers;

Who without spear, or sword, or other drum

Than what was in their tongue, did overcome;

And having conquer'd, did so strangely rule,

That the whole world did seem but the Pope's *mule.*

As new and old *Rome* did one empire twist;

So both together are one Antichrist;

Yet with two faces, as their *Janus* was,

Being in this their old crack'd looking-glass.

How dear to me, O God, thy counsels are! Who may with thee compare f Thus Sin triumphs in Western *Babylon;* Yet not as Sin, but as Religion. Of his two thrones he made the latter best, And to defray his journey from the East. Old and new *Babylon* are to hell and night, As is the Moon and Sun to Heaven and light. When the one did set, the other did take place, Confronting equally the Law and Grace. They are hell's landmarks, Satan's double crest: They are Sin's nipples, feeding th' east and west. But as in vice the Copy still exceeds The pattern, but not so in virtuous deeds; So though Sin made his latter seat the better, The latter Church is to the first a debtor. The second Temple could not reach the first: And the late reformation never durst

Compare with ancient times and purer years;

But in the Jews and us deserveth tears;

Nay, it shall every year decrease and fade;

Till such a darkness do the world invade

At Christ's last coming, as his first did find:

Yet must there such proportions be assign'd

To these diminishings, as is between

The spacious world and *Jewry* to be seen.

Religion stands on tiptoe in our land,

Ready to pass to the *American* strand.

When height of malice, and prodigious lusts,

Impudent sinning, witchcrafts, and distrusts,

(The marks of future bane), shall fill our cup

Unto the brim, and make our measure up;

When *Seine* shall swallow *Tiber,* and the *Thames,*

By letting in them both, pollutes her

streams:
When Italy of us shall have her will,
And all her Calendar of sins fulfil;
Whereby one may foretell, what sins next year
Shall both in *France* and *England* domineer:
Then shall Religion to *America* ilec:
They have their times of Gospel, even as we.
My God, thou dost prepare for them a way,
By carrying first their gold from them away:
For gold and grace did never yet agree:
Religion always sides with poverty.
We think we rob them, but we think amiss:
We arc more poor, and they more rich, by this.
Thou wilt revenge their quarrel, making grace
To pay our debts, and leave our ancient place
To go to them, while that, which now their nation
But lends to us, shall be our desolation.
Yet as the Church shall thither westward fly,
So Sin shall trace and dog her instantly:
They have their period also and set times
Both for their virtuous actions and their crimes.
And where of old the Empire and the Arts
Usher'd the Gospel ever in men's hearts, *Spain* hath done one; when Arts perform the other,
The Church shall come, and Sin the Church shall smother
That when they have accomplished the round,
And met in th' East their first and ancient sound,
Judgment may meet them both, and search them round.
Thus do both lights, as well in Church as Sun,
Light one another, and together run.
Thus also Sin and Darkness follow still
The Church and Sun with all their power and skill.
But as the Sim still goes both West and East:
So also did the Church by going West
Still Eastward go; because it drew more near
To time and place, where judgment shall appear.
How dear to me, 0 God, thy counsels are! Who may with thee compare f
L'ENVOY.
King of glory, King of peace,
With the one make war to cease;
With the other bless thy sheep,
Thee to love, in thee to sleep.
Let not Sin devour thy fold,
Bragging that thy blood is cold;
That thy death is also dead,
While his conquests daily spread;
That thy flesh hath lost his food,
And thy Cross is common wood.
o
Choke him, let him say no more, But reserve his breath in store, Till thy conquest and his fall Make his sighs to use it all; And then bargain with the wind To discharge what is behind.
Blessed he God alone,
Thrice blessed Three in One.
MISCELLANEOUS POEMS.
A SONNET, SENT BY GEORGE HERBERT TO IMS MOTHER AS A NEW YEAR'S GIFT FROM CAMBRIDGE.
My God, where is that ancient heat towards thee,
Wherewith whole shoals of Martyrs once did burn, Besides their other flames *l* Doth poetry
Wear Venus' livery? only serve her turn? Why arc not sonnets made of thec? and lays
Upon thine altar burnt *l* Cannot thy love Heighten a spirit to sound out thy praise
As well as any she *l* Caunot thy Dove Outstrip their *Cupid* easily in flight?
Or, since thy ways are deep, and still the same,
Will not a verse run smooth that bears thy name? Why doth that fire, which by thy power and might
Each breast does feci, no braver fuel choose
Than that which, one day, worms may chance refuse *l* Sure, Lord, there is enough in thee to dry
Oceans of ink; for, as the Deluge did
Cover the earth, so doth thy Majesty:
Each cloud distils thy praise, and doth forbid
Poets to turn it to another use.
Roses and lilies speak thee; and to make A pair of cheeks of them, is thy abuse.
"Why should I women's eyes for crystal tako? Such poor invention burns in their low mind
Whose fire is wild, and doth not upward go
To praise, and on thee, Lord, some ink bestow. Open the bones, and you shall nothing find
In the best face but filth; when, Lord, in thco
The beauty lies, in the discovery.
A PARADOX.
(FROM A MS. COLLECTION KORMFIII.V DR RAWUNSON'H, IN THE BODLEIAN LIlIUAUY, OXFORD.) THAT THE 8ICK ARE IN A BETTER CASE THAN THE WHOLE.
You who admire yourselves because
You neither groan nor weep,
And think it contrary to Nature's laws
To want one ounce of sleep,
Your strong belief
Acquits yourselves, and gives the sick all grief.
Your state to ours is contrary.
That makes you think us poor.
So Black-moors think us foul, and we
Arc quit with them, and more:
Nothing can see,
And judge of things but mediocrity.
The sick arc in themselves a state
Which health hath nought to do. How know you that our tears proceed from woe, And not from better fate '(Since that mirth hath
Her waters also and desired bath.
How know you that the sighs vc scnd
From want of breath proceed,
Not from excess? and therefore wc do spend
That which we do not need;
So trembling may
As well show inward warbling, as decay.
Cease then to judge calamities l'y outward form and show,
But view yourselves, and inward turn your eyes,
Then you shall fully know

That your estate
Is, of the two, the far more desperate.
  You always fear to feel those smarts
  Which we but sometimes prove,
  Each little comfort much affects our
hearts,
  None but gross joys you move:
  Why then confess
  Your fears in number more, your joys
arc less Then for yourselves not us em-
brace
Plaints to bad fortune due,
For though you visit us, and plaint or
case,
Wc doubt much whether you
Come to our bed
To comfort us, or to be comforted.

INSCRIPTION. IN THE PARSONAGE, BE-
MERTON. TO MY SUCCESSOR.

  If thou chance for to find
  A new House to thy mind
  And built without thy cost:
Be good to the poor,
As God gives thee store,
  And then my labour's not lost.

ON LORD DANVERS.

Sacred marble, safely keep
  His dust, who under thee must sleep,
  Until the years again restore
  Their dead, and time shall be no
more.
  Meanwhile, if ho (which all things
wears)
  Does ruin thee, or if thy tears
  Are shed for him; dissolve thy frame,
  Thou art requited: for his fame,
  His virtue, and his worth shall be
  Another monument to thee.

THE SYNAGOGUE; OR, THE SHADOW OF
THE TEMPLE: SACKED POEMS AND PRI-
VATE EJACULATIONS IN IMITATION OP
MR GEORGE HERBERT. BY CHRISTOPHER
IIAUVEY, M.A.

Stultissimum credo ad imitandum fion
optima qurrqnc proponcre.
  I'LIN. *Sec. Lib.* i. 1Cp. 5.
  I do esteem 't a folly uot the lc.it
To imitate examples not the!», t.
  Op Christopher Ilarvcy or lliirvie, the
author of the " Synagogue," all that is
known is, that he was a clergyman's son
in Cheshire, was educated at Brazcn-
Noso College, and became Vicar of
Clifton, Warwickshire. Ho published
tho "Synagogue" in 1C40, without his
name. Walton commended the book,
and ascribed it to Ilarvio. lie wroto another book called " Schola Cordis," so-
motimes ascribed to Quarlcs. His "Synagogue" has less poetic merit than tho
"Temple," but is very pious and instruc-
tive.

THE SYNAGOGUE. SUBTERLIMINARE.
*Die, cujiis Tcmplum f Christi. Quis con-
didit f Edc. Condidit* Ilcrbcrtus. *Die,
quibns auxiliis f
Auxiliis multis: quibus, hand mild di-
core fas est.
Tanta est ex dictis lis oriunda meis.
Gratia, si dicam, dedit omnia; protinus
obstat
Ingcnium, dicens, cuncta fuisse sua.
Ars negat, ct nihil est non not/rum dicit
in illo;
Nee facile est idem composuissc mihi.
Divide: mderiam del gratia, matcri-
aique
Ingcniujn cultus induat, arsque modus.
Non: ne displicetd pariter res omnibus
ista,
Nee sortita velint jura vocarc sua.
Ncmpc pari sibi jure pctunt, cult usque,
mudosque,
Materiami/uc, ars, ct gratia, ct ingcni-
um.
Erqo, velit si quis dubitantem tollerc
elenchum,
De Templo* Hcrbcrti *talia dicta dabit.
In Templo* Ilcrbcrtus *condendo est gra-
tia lotus,
Ars pariter totus, totus ct ingcnium.
Cedite Romanic, Graiiw quoqtic cedite
Musce;
Unumpar cunct'us Anglia jactat opus.*

A STEPPING-STONE TO THE THRESHOLD
OF MR HERBERT'S " CHURCH-PORCH."

  What Church is this? Christ's
Church. Who builded it?
  Master *George Herbert.* Who assist-
ed it?
  Many assisted: who I may not say,
  So much contention might arise that
way.
  If I say Grace gave all; Wit straight
doth thwart,
  And says, All that is there is mine:
but Art
  Denies, and says, There's nothing
there but's mine:
  Nor can I easily the right define.

Divide: say, Grace the matter gave,
and Wit
  Did polish it: Art measured, and
made fit,
  Each several piece, and framed it al-
together.
  No, by no means: this may not please
them neither.
  Nonc's well contented with a part
alone,
  When each doth challenge all to be
his own.
  The matter, the expressions, and the
measures,
  Are equally Art's, Wit's, and Grace's
treasures.
  Then he, that would impartially dis-
cuss
  This doubtful question, must answer
thus:
  In building of his Temple, Master
Herbert
  Is equally all grace, all wit, all art.
  Roman and Grecian Muses all give
way:
  One English Poem darkens all your
day.

THE DEDICATION.

Lord, my first fruits should have been
sent to thee;
  For thou the tree, That bare them, only lentest unto me.
  But while I had the use, the fruit was
mine: Not so divine
As that I dare presume to call it thine.
  Before 'twas ripe it fell unto the
ground: And since I found
It bruised in the dirt, nor clean, nor
sound.
  Some I have pick'd, and wiped, and
bring thee now,
  Lord, thou know'st how: Gladly I
would, but dare not it avow.
  Such as it is, 'tis here. Pardon the
best, Accept the rest.
Thy pardon and acceptance makcth
blest.

THE CHURCH-YARD.

  Thou that intendest to the Church to-
day,
Come, take a turn, or two, before thou
go'st,
In the Church-yard; the walk is in thy
way.
Who takes best heed in going, hastcth

most:
But he that unprepared rashly ventures,
Hastens perhaps to seal his death's in-
dentures.

THE CHURCH-STILE.

Seest thou that stile / Observe then
how it rises,
Step after step, and equally descends:
Such is the way to win Celestial prizes:
Humility the course begins, and ends.

Wouldst thou in grace to high perfections grow?

Shoot thy roots deep, ground thy
foundations low.

Humble thyself, and God will lift
thee up:

Those that exalt themselves he
casteth down:

The hungry he invites with him to
sup;

And clothes the naked with his robe
and crown.

Think not thou hast, what thou from
him wouldst have I lis labour's lost, if
thou thyself canst save.

Pride is the prodigality of grace,

Which casteth all away by griping all;

Humility is thrift, both keeps its
place,

And gains by giving, riseth by its fall.
To get by giving, and to lose by keeping, •
Is to be sad in mirth, and glad in weeping.

THE CHURCH-GATE.

Next to the stile, see where the gate
doth stand,
"Which, turning upon hooks and hinges
may
Easily be shut, or open'd with a hand:
Yet constant to its centre still doth stay;
And fetching a wide compass round
about,
Keeps the same course, and distance,
never out.

Such must the course be that to heav-
en tends;

He that the gates of righteousness
would enter,

Must still continue constant to his
ends,

And fix himself in God, as in his centre.

Cleave close to him by faith, then
move which way

Discretion leads thee, and thou shalt not
stray.

We never wander, till wo looso our
hold
Of him that is our way, our light, our
guide:
But, when we grow of our own strength
too bold,

Unhook'd from him, we quickly turn
aside,
lie holds us up, whilst in him we arc
found:
If once we fall from him, we go to
ground.

THE CHURCH-WALLS.

Now view the walls: the Church is
compass'd round.

As much for safety, as for ornament:
'Tis an inclosure, and no common
ground;

Tis God's freehold, and but our tene-
ment.
Tenants at will, and yet in tail, we be:
Our children have the same right to't as
we.

Remember there must be no gaps left
ope,
Where God hath fenced, for fear of false
illusions.
God will have all, or none: allows no
scope
For sin's encroachments, or men's own
intrusions.
Close binding locks his Laws together
fast:
lie that plucks out the first, pulls down
the last.

Either resolve for all, or else for
none;

Obedience universal he doth claim.

Either be wholly his, or all thine own:

At what thou canst not reach, at least
take aim:
lie that of purpose looks beside the
mark.
Might as well hood-wink'd shoot, or in
the dark.

THE CHURCH.

Lastly, consider where the Church
doth stand,
As near unto the middle as may be;
God in his service chiefly doth com-
mand
Above all other things sincerity.

Lines drawn from side to side within

a round,
Not meetiug in the centre, short are
found.

Religion must not side with any thing
That swerves from God, or else withdraws from him;

He that a welcome sacrifice would
bring,

Must fetch it from the bottom, not the
brim.
A sacred Temple of the Holy Ghost
Each part of man must be, but his heart
most.

Hypocrisy in Church is Alehemy,

That casts a golden tincture upon
brass:

There is no essence in it: 'tis a lie,

Though, fairly stamp'd, for truth it
ofcen pass:

Only the Spirit's *aqua rcgia* doth

Discover it to be but painted froth.

THE CHURCH-PORCH.

Now, ere thou passest further, sit thee
down
In the Church-porch, and think what
thou hast seen;
Let due consideration cither crown,
Or crush, thy former purposes. Between
Rash undertakings, and firm resolu-
tions,
Depends the strength, or weakness, of
conclusions.

Trace thy steps backward in thy
memory:
And first resolve of, what thou heardest
last,
Sincerity; It blots the history
Of all religious actions, and doth blast

The comfort of them, when in them
God sees

Nothing but outsides of formalities.

In earnest be religious, trifle not;

And rather for God's sake, than for
thine own:

Thou hast robb'd him, unless that he
have got

By giving, if his glory be not grown

Together with thy good: who seeketh
more
Himself than God, would make his roof
his floor..

Next to sincerity, remember still,

Thou must resolve upon integrity.

God will have all thou hast, thy mind,
thy will,

Thy thoughts, thy words, thy works. A nullity

It proves, when God, that should have all, doth find

That there is any one thing left behind.

And having given him all, thou must receive

All that he gives. Meet his Commandment:

Resolve that thine obedience must not leave,

Until it reach unto the same extent.

For all his Precepts arc of equal strength,

And measure thy performance to the length:

Then call to mind that constancy must knit

Thine undertakings and thine actions fast:

He that sets forth towards heaven, and doth sit

Down by the way, will be found short at last.

Be constant to the end, and thou shalt have

A heavenly garland, though an earthly grave.

But he that would be constant, must not take

Religion up by fits and starts alone;

But his continual practice must it make:

His course must be from end to end but one.

Bones often broken, and knit up again,

Lose of their length, though in their strength they gain.

Lastly, remember that Humility

Must solidate, and keep all close together.

What Pride puffs up with vain futility,

Lies open and exposed to all ill weather.

An empty bubble may fair colours carry;

But blow upon it, and it will not tarry.

Prize not thine own too high, nor undcr-rato

Another's worth; but deal indifferently:

View the defects of thy spiritual state,

And others' graces, with impartial eye.

Tho more thou decmest of thyself, the less

Esteem of thco will all men else ex-press.

Contract thy lesson now, and this is just

The sum of all. He that desires to see

The face of God, in his Religion must

Sincere, entire, constant, and humble be.

If thus resolved, fear not to proceed:

Else tho more haste thou makest, the worse thou'lt speed.

CHURCH-UTENSILS.

Betwixt two dangerous rocks, Profaneness on

The one side, on the other Superstition,

How shall I sail secure?

Lord, be my 6tccrsman, hold my helm,

And then though winds with waves o'crwhelm

My sails, I will endure

It patiently. The bottom of the sea

Is safe enough, if thou direct the way.

I'll tug my tacklings then, I'll ply mine oars,

And cry, A fig for fear. lie that adores

The giddy multitude

So much, as to despise my rhymes,

Because they tunc not to the times,

I wish may not intrude

His presence here. But they (and that's enough)

Who love God's house, will like his household stud,.

THE FONT.

The Font, I say. Why not? And why not near

To the Church door? Why not of stone?

Is not that blessed fountain open'd here,

From whence that water flows alone,

Which from sin and uncleaimess washcth clear?

And may not beggars well contented be

Their first alms at the door to take?

Though, when acquainted better, they may see

Others within that bolder make.

Low places will serve guests of low degree.

What? Is he not the rock, out of whose side

Those streams of water-blood run forth?

The elect and precious corner-stone well tried?

Though the odds be great between their worth,

Rock-water and stone vessels are allied.

But call it what, and place it where you will:

Let it be made indifferently Of any form, or matter; yet, until

The blessed Sacrament thereby Impaired be, my hopes you shall not kill, p

To want a complement of comeliness Some of my comfort may abate,

And for the present make my joy go less:

Yet I will hug mine homely state,

And poverty with patience richly dress.

Regeneration is all in all;

Washing, or sprinkling, but the sign, The seal, and instrument thereof; I call

The one, as well as the other, mine, And my posterity's, as federal.

If temporal estates may be convey'd, By covenants on condition,

To men, and to their heirs; be not afraid, My soul, to rest upon

The covenant of grace by mercy made.

Do but thy duty, and rely upon't, Repentance, faith, obedience,

Whenever practised truly, will amount

To an authentic evidence,

Though the deed were antedated at tho Pont.

THE READING-PEW.

Here my new cntcr'd soul doth first break fast, Here scascneth her infant taste,

And at her mother-nurse the Church's dugs

With labouring lips and tongue she tugs,

For that sincere milk, which alone doth feed

Babes new-born of immortal seed:

Who, that they may unto perfection grow,

Must bo content to creep before they go.

They, that would reading out of Church exclude, Sure have a purpose to obtrude

Some dictates of their own, instead of God's

Revealed Will, his Word. Tis odds,

They do not mean to pay men current coin,

Who seek the standard to purloin,

And would reduce all trials to their own,
But touch-stones, balances, and weights, alone.

What reasonable man would not mis-doubt

Those Comments, that the text leave out /

And that their main intent is alter-ation,
Who dote so much on variation,

That no set Forms at all they can en-dure
To be prescribed, or put in urc /

Rejecting bounds and limits is the way,

If not all waste, yet common all to lay.

But why should he, that thinks him-self well grown, Be discontent that such a one,
As knows himself an infant yet, should be
Dandled upon his mother's knee,
And babe-like fed with milk, till he have got
More strength and stomach / Why should not
Nurslings in Church, as well as wean-lings, find
Their food fit for them in their proper kind?

Let them that would build castles in the air,
Vault thither, without step or stair;

Instead of feet to climb, take wings to fly,
And think their turrets top the sky.

But let mo lay all my foundations deep,
And learn, before I run, to creep.
Who digs through Rocks to lay his ground-works low,
May in good time build high, and sure, though slow.

To take degrees, *per saltum,* though of quick Dispatch, is but a truant's trick.
Let us learn first to know our letters well,
Then syllables, then words to spell;
Then to read plainly, cro wo tako the pen
In hand to write to other men.
I doubt their preaching is not always true,
Whoso way to the Pulpit's not the ltcad-ing-pcw.

THE BOOK OF COMMON PRAYER.

What I Prayer by the book? and Com-mon?
Yes. Why not?
The spirit of grace,
And supplication,
Is not left free alone
For time and place;
But manner too. To read, or speak by rote
Is all alike to him that prays
With 'b heart, that with his mouth ho says.
They that in private by themselves alone
Do pray, may tako
What liberty they please,
In choosing of the ways,
Wherein to make

Their soul's most intimate affections known
To him that sees in secret, when
They arc most conccal'd from other men.

But he, that unto others leads the way
In public prayer,
Should choose to do it so,
As all, that hear, may know
They need not fear
To tunc their hearts unto his tongue, and say
Amen; nor doubt they were bctray'd
To blaspheme, when they should have pray'd.

Devotion will add life unto the letter.
And why should not
That, which Authority
Prescribes, esteemed be
Advantage rot?
If the Prayer be good, the commoner, the better.
Prayer in the Church's words, as well
As sense, of all prayers bears the bell.

THE BIBLE.

The Bible? That's the Book. The Book indeed,
The Book of Books;
On which who looks,
As he should do, aright, shall never need
Wish for a better light
' To guide him in the night:

Or, when ho hungry is, for bettor food
To feed upon,

Than this alone,
If ho bring stomach and digestion good:
And if he bo amiss,
This the best Physic is.

The true Panchreston 'tis for every soro
And sickness, which
The poor, and rich
With equal case may come by. Yea, 'tis more,
An antidote, as well
As remedy 'gainst Hell.

'Tis Heaven in perspective, and the bliss
Of glory here,
If any where,
By Saints on Earth anticipated is,
Whilst faith to every word
A bcin' doth afford.

It is the Looking-glass of souls, wherein
All men may see,
Whether they be
Still, as by nature they are, deform'd with sin;
Or in a better case,
As new adorn'd with grace.

'Tis the great Magazine of spiritual arms,
Wherein doth lie
The artillery
Of Heaven, ready charged against all harms,
That might come by the blows
Of our infernal foes.

God's Cabinet of revealed counsel 'tis:
Where weal and woo
Arc ordcr'd so,
That every man may know which shall be his;
Unless his own mistake
False application make.

It is the Index to Eternity.
lie cannot miss
Of endless bliss,
That takes this chart to steer his voyage by.
Nor can he bo mistook,
That spcakcth by this Book.

A Book, to which no Book may be com-pared
For excellence;
Pre-eminence
Is proper to it, and cannot be shared.

Divinity alone
Belongs to it, or none.
   It is the Book of God. What if I should
Say, God of Books /
Let him that looks
Angry at that expression, as too bold,
   His thoughts in silence smother,
Till he find such another.

THE TULPIT.

   'Tis dinner time: and now I look For a full meal. God send me a good Cook:
   This is the dresser-board, and here I wait in expectation of good cheer.
   I'm sure the Master of the house
Enough to entertain his guests allows:
And not enough of sonic one sort alone,
But choice of what best fitteth every one.
God grant mc taste and stomach good:
My feeding will diversify my food;
'Tis a good appetite to cat,
And good digestion, that makes good meat.
The best food in itself will be,
Not fed on well, poison, not food, to me.
Let him that speaks look to his words; my car
Must carcfid be, both what and how I hear.
'Tis *Manna* that I look for here,
The bread of Heaven, Angels' food. I fear
No want of plenty, where I know
The loaves by eating, more, and greater, grow;
Where nothing but forbearance makes
A famine; where he only wants, that takes
Not what he will; provided that he would
Take nothing to himself, but what he should.
Here the same fountain pourcth forth
Water, Wine, Milk, Oil, Honey, and the worth
Of all transcendent, infinite
In excellence, and to each appetite
In fitness answerable; so
That none needs hence unsatisfied go,
Whose stomach serves him unto any thing,
That health, strength, comfort, or content can bring.
Yea, dead men here invited are
Unto the bread of life, and whilst they spare
To come and take it, they must blame
Themselves, if thcy continue still the same.
The body's fed by food, which it
Assimilates, and to itself doth fit:
But, that the soul may feed, itself must be
Transformed to the Word, with it agree.
To milk the strongest men must bo
As new-born babes, whenever they it see,
Desiring, not despising it.
For strong meat babes must stay, and strive to fit
Themselves in time, until thcy can
Get by degrees (which best beseem a man)
Experience-exercised senses, able
Good to discern from evil, truth from fable.
Here I will wait then; till I see
The steward reaching out a mess for me:
Resolve I'll take it thankfully, Whatc'cr it be, and feed on't heartily.
Although no *Benjamin's* choice mess,
Five times as much as others, but far less;
Yea, if it be but a basket full of crumbs,
I'll bless the hand, from which, by which, it comes.
Like an invited guest, I will
Be bold, but mannerly withal, sit still
And see what the Master of the feast
Will carve unto me, and account that best
Which he doth choose for me, not I Myself desire: yea, though I should espy
Some fault iu the dressing, in the disliiug, or The placing, yet I will not it abhor.
   So that the meat be wholesome, though The sauce shall not bo toothsome, I'll not go
   Empty away, and starve my soul, To feed my foolish fancy; but control
   My appetite to dainty things, Which oft instead of strength diseases brings:
But, if my Pulpit-hopes shall all prove vain, I'll back unto the Reading-pew again.

THE COMMUNION TABLE.

Here stands my banquet ready, the last course,
And best provision,
That I must feed upon,
   Till death my soul and body shall divorce,
And that I am
   Call'd to the marriage-supper of the Lamb.
   Some call't the Altar, some the holy Table.
The name I stick not at,
Whether't be this, or that,
   I care not much, so that I may be able
Truly to know
   Both why it is, and may be called so.
   And for the matter whereof it is made,
The matter is not much,
Although it be of tuch,
   Or wood, or metal, what will last, or fade;
So vanity
   And superstition avoided be.
   ' Tuch:' old word for cloth.
   Nor would it trouble me to see it found
Of any fashion,
That can be thought upon,
   Square, oval, many-angled, long, or round:
If close it be,
   Fix'd, open, moveable, all's one to me.
   And yet, mcthinks, at a Communion
   In uniformity There's greatest decency,
And that which makcth most for union:
But needlessly
To vary, tends to the breach of charity.
   Yet, rather than I'll give, I will not take
   Offence, if it be given, So that 1 be not driven
To thwart authority, a party make
For faction,
Or side, but seemingly, in the action.
   At a Communion I wish I might
   Have no cause to suspect
Any, the least, defect
   Of unity and peace, either in sight
Apparently,
   Or in men's hearts concealed secretly.
   That, which ordained is *to* make men one,
More than before they were,

Should not itself appear,
   Though but appear, distinctly di-
verse. None
Too much can see
   Of what, when most, yet but enough
can be.
   If others will dissent, and vary, who
Can help it? If I may,
As hath been done alway,
   By the best, and most; I will myself
do so.
Of one accord
   The servants should be of one God,
one Lord.

COMMUNION PLATE.

Never was gold, or silver, graced thus
Before.
To bring this body, and this blood, to us
Is more
Than to crown Kings,
Or be made rings,
For star-like diamonds to glitter in.
   No precious stones are meet to match
this bread Divine.
Spirits of pearls dissolved would but
dead
This wine.
This heavenly food
Is too too good
To be compared to any earthly thing.
   For such inestimable treasure can
There bo
Vessels too costly made by any man?
Sure ho
That knows the meat
So good to eat,
Would wish to see it richly served in.
   Although 'tis true, that sanctity's not
tied To state,
Yet sure Religion should not be envied
The fate
Of meaner worth,
To be set forth
As best becomes the service of a King.
   A King unto whose cross all Kings
must vail Their crowns,
And at his beck in their full course
strike sail:
Whose frowns
And smiles give date
Unto their fate,
And doom them, either unto weal, or
woe.
   A King, whose will is justice: and
whose word.

Is power,
And wisdom both. A King, whom to af-
ford
An hour
Of service truly
Perform'd, and duly,
Is to bespeak eternity of bliss.
When such a King offers to come to mc
As food,
Shall I suppose his carriages can be
Too good *I*
No: Stars to gold
Turn'd, never could
Be rich enough to be employ'd so.
   If I might wish then, I would have
this bread,
   This wine,
   Vesseird in what the Sun might blush
to shed His shine.
When he should see:
But, till that be,
   I'll rest contented with it, as it is.

CHURCH-OFFICERS.

Stay. Officers in Church? Take heed: it
is
   A tender matter to bo touch'd. If I
chance to say any thing amiss,
   Which is not fit to be avouch'd, I
must expect whole swarms of wasps to
sting me, Few, or no bees, honey or
wax, to bring me.
   Some would have none in Church do
any thing As Officers, but gifted men;
Others into the number more would
bring,
Than I see warrant for: So then,
All that I say, 'tis like, will censured be,
Through prejudice, or partiality.
   But 'tis no matter; If men censure me,
They but my fellow-servants are:
   Our Lord allows us all like liberty.
   I write, mine own thoughts to declare,
   Not to please men: and, if I displease
any, 1 will not care, so they bo of the
Many.

THE SEXTON.

The Church's kcy-keepcr opens the
door, And shuts it, sweeps the floor,
Rings bells, digs graves, and fills them
up again;
All Emblems unto men,
Openly owning Christianity,
To mark, and learn many good lessons
by.
0 thou that hast the key of *David*, who

Open'st and shuttest so,
That none can shut or open after thee,
Vouchsafe thyself to be
Our soul's door-keeper, by thy blessed
Spirit:
The lock and key's thy mercy, not our
merit.
   Cleanse thou our sin-soil'd souls
from the dirt and dust Of every noisome
lust,
Brought in by the foul feet of our atfec-
tions:
The besom of afflictions,
With the blessing of thy Spirit added to
it,
If thou be pleased to say it shall, will do
it.
   Lord, ringing changes all our bells
hath marr'd, Jangled they have, and
jarr'd
So long, they're out of tune, and out of
frame,
They seem not now the same.
Put them in frame anew, and once begin
To tune them so, that they may chime
all in.
   Let all our sins be buried in thy grave,
' No longer rant and rave,
   As they have done, to our eternal
shame,
And the scandal of thy name.
Let's as door-keepers in thine house at-
tend,
Rather than the throne of wickedness
ascend.

THE CLERK.

The Church's Bible-Clerk attends
Her Utensils, and ends
Her Prayers with Amen;
Tunes Psalms, and to the Sacraments
Brings in the Elements,
And takes them out again;
Is humble-minded, and industrious
handed,
Doth nothing of himself, but as com-
manded.
All that the Vessels of the Lord
Do bear with one accord
Must study to be pure,
As they are: if his holy eye
Do any spot espy,
He cannot it endure;
But most cxpcctcth to be sanctified
In those come nearest him, and glori-
fied.

Psalms then are always tuned best,
When there is most exprest
The holy Penman's heart:
All Music is but discord where
That wants, or doth not bear
The first and chiefest part.
Voices, without affections answerable,
When best, to God arc most abomin-
able.
Though in the blessed Sacraments
The outward Elements
Arc but as husks and shells;
Yet ho that knows the kernel's worth,
If even those send forth
Some Aromatic smells,
Will not esteem it waste, lest, Judas-
like,
Through *Mary's* side he Christ himself
should strike.
Lord, without whom we cannot tell
How to speak or think, well,
Lend us thy helping hand,
That what we do may pleasing be,
Not to ourselves but thee,
And answer thy command:
So that, not we alone, but thou may'st
say
Amen to all our prayers, pray'd the right
way.

THE OVERSEER OF THE POOR.
The Church's Almoner takes care, that
none
In their necessity Shall unprovided
bo
Of maintenance, or employment; those
alono,
Whom careless Idleness, Or riotous
excess,
Condemns to needless want, he leaves
to be
Chasten'd a while by their own poverty.
Thou gracious Lord, rich in thyself,
dost give
To all men liberally,
Upbraiding none. Thine eye
Is open upon all. In thee we live,
Q
We move, and have our being:
But there is more than seeing.
For the poor with thee: they are thy
special charge;
To them thou dost thine heart and
hand enlarge.
Four sorts of poor there are, with
whom thou dcal'st.

Though always differently, With
such indiffcrency,
That none hath reason to complain: thou
hcal'st
All those whom thou dost wound: If
there be any found
Hurt by themselves, thou ieavest them
to enduro
The pain, till the pain render them fit for
cure.
Some in the world are poor, but rich
in faith:
Their outward poverty A plentiful
supply
Of inward comforts and contentments
hath.
And their estate is blest, In this above
the rest,
It was thy choice, whilst thou on earth
didst stay,
And hadat not whereupon thy head to
lay.
Some poor in spirit in the world are
rich,
Although not many such:
And no man needs to grutch
Their happiness, who to maintain that
pitch,
Have a hard task in hand,
Nor easily can withstand
' The strong temptations that attend
on riches: Mountains are more exposed
to storms than ditches.
Some rich in the world are spiritually
poor,
And destitute of grace,
Who may perchance have placo In
the Church upon earth; but Heaven's
door
Too narrow is to admit Such camels
in at it.
Till they sell all they have, that field to
buy,
Wherein the true treasure doth hidden
lie.
Some spiritually poor, and destitute
Of grace in the world are poor,
Begging from door to door, Accursed
both in God's and man's repute,
Till by their miseries
Tutor'd they learn to prize Hungering
and thirsting after righteousness, Whilst
they're on earth, their greatest happi-
ness.
Lord, make me poor in spirit, and re-

lieve
Me how thou wilt thyself, No want of
worldly pelf
Shall make me discontented, fret and
grieve.
I know thine alius arc best:
But, above all the rest, Condemn me
not unto the hell of riches, Without thy
grace to countercrarm the witches.

THE CHURCH-WARDEN.
The Church's guardian takes care to
keep
Her buildings always in repair,
Unwilling that any decay should
creep
On them, before he is aware.
Nothing defaced,
Nothing displaced lie likes; but most
doth long and love to sco The living
stones order'd as they should be.
Lord, thou not only supervisor art
Of all our works, but in all those,
Which wo dare own, thine is the
chiefest part; For there is none of us,
that knows How to do well; Nor can wc
tell What we should do, unless by thee
directed: It prospers not that's by our-
selves projected.
That which wc think ourselves to
mend, wc mar, And often make it ten
times worse:
Reforming of Religion by war
Is the chymic blessing of a curse.
Great odds it is
That we shall miss
Of what we looked for: Thine ends can-
not
By any but by thine own means be got.
'Tis strange we so much dote upon
our own
Deformity, and others scorn; As if
ourselves were beautiful alone;
When that which did us most adorn
Wc purposely Choose to lay by, Such
decency and order, as did place us In
highest esteem, and guard as well as
grace us.
Is not thy daughter glorious within,
When clothed in ncedlc-work with-
out *l*
Or is't not rather both their shame
and sin,
That change her robe into a clout,
Too narrow, and Too thin, to stand
Her need in any stead, much less to be

An ornament fit for her high degree?

Take pity on her, Lord, and heal her breaches; Clothe all her enemies with shame:
All the despite that's done unto her reaches
To the dishonour of thy name.
Make all her sons
Rich precious stones,
To shine each of them in his proper place,
Receiving of thy fulness grace for grace.

THE DEACOX.

The Deacon! That's the Minister.
True, taken generally;
And without any sinister
Intent, used specially.
He's purposely ordain'd to minister.
In sacred things, to another officer.
At whose appointment, in whose stead, lie doth what he should do, In some things, not in all: is led By Law, and custom too. Where that doth neither bid, nor forbid, ho Thinks this sufficient authority:
Loves not to vary, when he sees
No great necessity;
To what's commanded he agrees,
With all humility;
Knowing how highly God submission prizes,
Pleased with obedience more than sacrifices.
Lord, thou didst of thyself profess
Thou wast as one that served.
And freely choosest to go less,
Though none so much deserved.
With what face can we then refuse to be
Enter'd thy servants in a low degree 1
Thy way to exaltation Was by humility;
But we, proud generation,
No difference of degree
In holy orders will allow, nay, more,
All holy orders would turn out of door.
But, if thy precept cannot do't.
To make us humbly serve,
Nor thy example added to't,
If still from both we swerve,
Let none of us proceed, till he can tell,
I low to uso the ofiico of a Deacon well.
Which by tho blessing of thy Spirit,
Whom thou hast left to bo Thy Vicar here, we may inherit, And minister to thee, Though not so well as thou may'st well expect, Yet so, as thou wilt pleased be to accept.

THE PRIEST.

The Priest, I say, the Presbyter, I mean, As now-a-days he's call'd
By many men: but I choose to retain
The name wherewith iustall'd
He was at first in our own mother tongue:
And doing so, I hope, I do no wrong.
The Priest, I say, 'a a middle Officer, Between the Bishop and
The Deacon; as a middle offerer.
Which in the Church doth stand
Between God and the people, ready press'd
In the behalf of both to do his best.
From him to them offers the promises Of mercy which he makes;
For them to him doth all their faults confess,
Their prayers and praises takes;
And offers for them, at the throne of grace,
Contentedly attending his own place.
The Word and Sacraments, the means of grace, He duly doth dispense,
The flourishes of falsehood to deface,
With truth's clear evidence;
And sin's usurped tyranny suppress,
By advancing righteousness, and holiness.
The public censures of the Church he sees
To execution brought: But nothing rashly of himself decrees,
Nor covets to be thought Wiser than his superiors; whom always He actively, or passively, obeys.
Lord Jesus, thou the Mediator art Of the new Testameut,
And fully didst perform thy double part Of God and man, when sent
To reconcile the world, and to atone
Twixt it and heaven, of two making one.
Yea, after the order of Mclehisedcck,
Thou art a Priest for ever.
With perfect righteousness thyself dost deck.
Such as decayeth never.
Like to thyself make all thy Priests on earth,
Bless'd fathers to thy sons of the second birth.

Thou earnest to do the will of him that sent thee,
And didst his honour seek
More than thine own: well may it then repent thee,
Being thyself so meek,
To have admitted them into the place
Of sons, that seek their fathers to disgrace.
Lord, grant that the abuse may be reform'd, Before it ruin bring
Upon thy poor despised Church, transform'd
As if 'twere no such thing:
Thou that the God of order art, and peace,
Make cursed confusion and contention cease.

Tub Bishop.

The Bishop / Yes, why not / What doth that name
Import that is unlawful, or unfit /
To say the Overseer is the same
In substance, and no hurt, I hope, in it:
But sure if men did not despise the thing,
Such scorn upon the name they would not fling.
Some Priests, some Presbyters, I mean, would be
Each Overseer of his several cure;
But one Superior, to oversee
Them altogether, they will not endure:
This the main difference is, that I can see,
Bishops they would not have, but they would be.
But who can show of old that ever any
Presbyteries without their Bishops were:
Though Bishops without Presbyteries many,
At first must needs be, almost every where /
That Presbyters from Bishops first arose,
To assist them, 's probable, not these from those.
However, a true Bishop I esteem
The highest Officer the Church on earth
Can have, as proper to itself, and

deem

A Church without one an imperfect
birth,
If constituted so at first, and maim'd,
If whom it had, it afterwards disclaim'd.

All order first from unity ariseth,
And th' essence of it is subordination:
Whoever this contemns, and that de-
spiseth,
May talk of, but intends not, reforma-
tion.

'Tis not of God, of Nature, or of Art,
To ascribe to all what's proper to one
part.

To rule and to be ruled are distinct,
And several duties, severally belong
To several persons, can no more be
link'd
In altogether, than amidst the throng
Of rude unruly passions, in the heart,
Reason can see to act her sovereign
part.

But a good Bishop, as a tender father,
Doth teach and rule the Church, and is
oboy'd;
And reverenced by it, so much the
rather,
By how much he delighted more to lead
All by his own example in the way,
Than punish any, when they go astray.

Lord, thou the Bishop, and chief
Shepherd, art
Of all that flock, which thou hast pur-
chased
With thine own blood: to them thou dost
impart
The benefits which thou hast merited,

Teaching, and ruling, by thy blessed
Spirit,
Their souls in grace, till glory they in-
herit:

The stars which thou dost hold in thy
right hand,

The Angels of the Churches, Lord,
direct

Clearly thy holy will to understand,
And do accordingly: Let no defect
Nor fault, no not in our new politics,
Provoke thee to remove our candle-
sticks;

But let thy Urim and thy Thummim
be
Garments of praise to adorn thine holy
ones:
Light and perfection let all men see

Brightly shine forth in those rich pre-
cious stones;
Of whom thou wilt mako a foundation,
To raise thy new llicrusalera upon.

And, at the brightness of its rising, let
All nations with thy people shout for
joy:

Salvation for walls and bulwarks set
About it, that nothing may it annoy.

Then the whole world thy Diocess
shall be, And Bishops all but Suffragans
to Thee.

CHURCH FESTIVALS.
Marrow of time, Eternity in brief
Compendiums Epitomized, the chief
Contents, the Indices, the Title-pages
Of all past, present, and succeeding
ages,
Sublimate graces, antedated glories,

The cream of holiness,
The inventories
Of future blessedness,
The Florilegia of celestial stories,
Spirits of joys, the relishes and closes
Of Angels' music, pearls dissolved, ros-
es
Perfumed, sugar'd honey-combs, de-
lights

Never too highly prized,
The marriage rites,
"Which duly solemnized
Usher espoused souls to bridal nights.
Gilded sunbeams, refined Elixirs,
And quintessential extracts of stars:
Who loves not you, doth but in vain pro-
fess
That ho loves God, or heaven, or happi-
ness.

THE SABBATH, OR LORD'S DAY.
Hail
Holy
King of days,
The Emperor,
Or Universal
Monarch of time, the week's
Perpetual Dictator.
Thy
Beauty
Far exceeds
The reach of art,
To blazon fully;
And I thy light eclipse,
When I most strive to raise thee.
What
Nothing

Else can be,
Thou only art;
Tli' extracted spirit
Of all Eternity,
By favour antedated.
Vail
Wholly
To thy praise,
For evermore
Must the rehearsal
Of all, that honour seeks,
Under the world's Creator.
My
Duty
Yet must needs
Yield thee mine heart,
And that not dully:
Spirits of souls, not lips
Alone, arc fit to praise 0
That I
Could lay by
This body so,
That my soul might be
Incorporate with thee,
And no more to six days owe.

THE ANNUNCIATION", OR LADY-DAY.
Unto the music of the spheres
Let men, and Angels, join in concert
theirs.
So great a messenger
From heaven to carth
Is seldom seen,
Attired in so much glory;
A message wcleomer,
Fraught with more mirth,
Hath never been
Subject of any story:
This by a double right, if any, may
Be truly styled the world's birth-day.
The making of the world ne'er cost
So dear, by much, as to redeem it lost.
God said but, *Let it be,*
And every thing
Was made straightway,
So as he saw it good:
But ere that he could sec
A course to bring
Man gone astray
To the place where he stood,
His wisdom with his mercy, for man's
sake,
Against his justice part did take.
And the result was this day's news
Able the messenger himself to amuse,
As well as her, to whom

By him 'twas told,
That though she were
A Virgin pure, and knew
No man, yet in her womb
A son she should
Conceive and bear,
As sure as God was true.
Such high place in his favour she possess'd,
Being among all women bless'd.
But bless'd especially in this,
That she believed, and for eternal bliss
Relied on him, whom she
Herself should bear,
And her own son
Took for her Saviour.
And if there any be,
That when they hear,
As she had done,
Suit their behaviour,
They may be blessed, as she was, and say,
'Tis their Annunciation-day.

THE NATIVITY, OR CHRISTMAS-DAY.
Unfold thy face, unmask thy ray,
    Shine forth bright sun, double the day.
    Let no malignant misty fume,
    Nor foggy vapour, once presume
    To interpose thy perfect sight
    This day, which makes us love thy light
    For ever better, that we could
    That blessed object once behold,
    Which is both the circumference,
    And centre of all excellence:
    Or rather neither, but a treasure
    Unconfined without measure,
    Whose centre, and circumference,
    Including all pre-eminence,
    Excluding nothing but defect,
    And infinite in each respect,
    Is equally both here and there,
    And now, and then, and every where,
    And always, one, himself, the same,
    A being far above a name.
    Draw nearer then, and freely pour
    Forth all thy light into that hour,
    Which was crowned with his birth,
    And made heaven envy earth.
    Let not his birth-day clouded be,
By whom thou shinest, and we see.

THE CIRCUMCISION, OR NEW-YEAR'S DAY.
    Sorrow betide my sins I Must smart

so soon
Seize on my Saviour's tender flesh scarce grown
    Unto an eighth day's age / Can nothing else assuage
The wrath of heaven, but his infant-blood /
Innocent Infant, infinitely good!
    Is this thy welcome to the world, great God!
No sooner born, but subject to the rod
    Of sin-incensed wrath?
Alas! what pleasure hath
Thy Father's justice to begin thy passion,
Almost together with thine incarnation?
Is it to antedate thy death / to indite
Thy condemnation himself, and write
    The copy with thy blood,
    Since nothing is so good? Or, is't by this experiment to try, Whether thou beest born mortal, and canst die?
    If man must needs draw blood of God, yet why
    Stays he not till thy time be come to die?
Didst thou thus early bleed
For us to show what need
    We have to hasten unto thee as fast;
    And learn that all the time is lost that's pass'd?
'Tis true, we should do so: Yet in this blood
There's something else, that must be understood;
It seals thy covenant,
That so we may not want
Witness enough against thee, that thou art
Made subject to the Law, to act our part.
    The sacrament of thy regeneration
It cannot be; it gives no intimation
    Of what thou wort, but we: Native impurity;
Original corruption, was not thine,
But only as thy righteousness is mine.
    In holy Baptism this is brought to me,
As that in Circumeision was to thee:
So that thy loss and pain
Do prove my joy and gain.
Thy Circumeision writ thy death in blood:
Baptism in water seals my livelihood.
0 blessed change! Yet, rightly understood, That blood was water, and this

water 's blood.
    What shall I give again, To recompense thy pain?
Lord, take reveuge upon me for this smart:
To quit thy fore-skin, circumeise my heart.

THE EPIPHANY, OR TWELFTH-DAY.
    Great, without controversy great,
They that do know it will confess
The mystery of godliness;
    Whereof the Gospel doth intreat.
    God in the flesh is manifest,
    And that which hath for ever been
Invisible, may now be seen,
    The eternal Deity new drest.
    Angels to shepherds brought the news:
And Wise men, guided by a Star,
To seek the Sun, are come from far:
    Gentiles have got the start of Jews.
    The stable and the manger hide
His glory from his own; but these
Though strangers, his resplendent rays
    Of Majesty divine have spied.
    Gold, frankincense, and myrrh, they give;
And worshipping him plainly show,
That unto him they all things owe,
    By whose free gift it is they live.
it
    Though clouded in a veil of flesh,
The Sun of Righteousness appears,
Melting cold cares, and frosty fears,
    And making joys spring up afresh.
0 that his light and influence,
Would work effectually in mo
Another new Epiphany,
Exhale, and elevate me hence:
    That, as my calling doth requiro,
Star-like I may to others shine;
And guide them to that Sun divine,
    Whose day-light never shall expire l

THE PASSION, OR GOOD FRIDAY.
    This day my Saviour died: and do I live?
What, hath not sorrow slain me yet /
Did the immortal God vouchsafe to give
His life for mine, and do I set
More by my wretched life, than ho by his,
So full of glory, and of bliss?
    Did his free mercy, and mere love to me,
Make him forsake his glorious throne,

And mount a cross, the stage of in-
famy,
That so he might not die alone;
   But dying suffer more through grief
and shame,
Thau mortal men havo power to namo?
   And can ingratitude Bo far prevail,
   To keep mo living still *i.* Alas! Mc-
thiuks some thorn out of his crown,
some nail,
   At least his spear, might pierce, and
pass Thorough, and thorough, till it
rived mine heart,
   As the right death-deserving part.
   And doth he not expect it should be
so *l* Would he lay down a price so great,
And not look that his purchases should
grow
Accordingly? Shall I defeat
His just desire *l* 0 no, it cannot be:
   His death must needs be death to me.
   My life's not mine, but his: for he did
die That I might live: yet died so,
That being dead he was alive; and I
Thorough the gates of death must go
To live with him: yea, to live by him
here
   Is a part in his death to bear.
   Die then, dull soul, and if thou canst
not die,
   Dissolve thyself into a Sea Of living
tears, whose streams may ne'er go dry,.
   Nor turned be another way, Till they
have drown'd all joys, but those alone,
   Which sorrow claimeth for its own.
   For sorrow hath its joys: and I am
glad That I would grieve, if I do not:
But, if I neither could, nor would, be sad
And sorrowful, this day, my lot
Would be to grieve for ever, with a grief
   Uncapable of all relief.
   No grief was like that,-which he
grieved for me,
A greater grief than can be told:
   And liko my grief for him no grief
should be,
If I could grieve so, as I would:
   But what I would, and cannot, ho
doth sco,
And will accept, that died for me.
   Lord, as thy grief and death for me
arc mine,
For thou hast given them unto mo;
   So my desires to grievo and die arc
thine,

For they arc wrought only by thee.
   Not for my sake then, but thine own,
bo pleased
With that, which thou thyself hast
raised.

THE RESURRECTION, OR EASTER-DAY.

   Up, and away,
   Thy Saviour's gone before. Why dost
thou stay,
   Dull soul? Behold, the door Is open,
and his Precept bids thee rise, Whose
power hath vanquish'd all thine enemies.
   Say not, I live,
   Whilst in the grave thou liest: He that
doth give
   Thee life would have thee prize't
More highly than to keep it buried,
where Thou canst not make the fruits of
it appear.
   Is rottenness,
   And dust so pleasant to thee, That
happiness,
   And heaven, cannot woo thee, To
shako thy shackles off, and leave bchind
thco Those fetters, which to death and
hell do bind thco *l*
   In vain thou say'st, Thou art buried
with thy Saviour,
If thou dclay'st,
To show, by thy behaviour,
That thou art risen with him; Till thou
shine
Like him, how canst thou say his light is
thine?
   Early he rose, And with him brought
the day,
Which all thy foes
Frighted out of the way:
And wilt thou sluggard-like turn in thy
bed,
Till noon-sun beams draw up thy
drowsy head?
   Open thine eyes,
   Sin-seized soul, and see What cob-
web-ties
   They are, that trammel thee; Not
profits, pleasures, honours, as thou
thinkest; But loss, pain, shame, at which
thou vainly winkest.
   All that is good Thy Saviour dearly
bought
With his heart's blood;
And it must there be sought,
Where he keeps residence, who rose

this day:
Linger no longer then; up, and away.
THE ASCENSION, OR HOLY THURSDAY.
   Mount, mount, my soul, and climb, or
rather fly
With all thy force on high,
   Thy Saviour rose not only, but as-
cended;
And he must be attended
   Both in his conquest and his triumph
too.
His glories strongly woo
   His graces to them, and will not ap-
pear
   In their full lustre, until both be there,
   Whcro ho now sits, not for himself
alone,
   But that upon his throne All his re-
deemed may attendants bo
   Robed, and crown'd as he. Kings
without Courtiers arc lone men, they
say;
   And dost thou think to stay Behind on
earth, whilst thy King reigns in heaven,
Yet not bo of thy happiness bcrcaven?
   Nothing that thou canst think worth
having 's here.
Nothing is wanting there,
That thou canst wish, to make thee truly
blest.
And, above all the rest,
Thy life is hid with God in Jesus Christ,
Higher than what is high'st.
0 grovel then no longer hero on earth,
Where misery every moment drowns
thy mirth.
But tower, my soul, and soar above the
skies,
Where thy true treasure lies.
   Though with corruption and mortali-
ty
   Thou clogg'd and pinion'd be;
   Yet thy fleet thoughts, and sprightly
wishes, may Speedily glide away.
   To what thou canst not reach, at least
aspire,
   Ascend, if not in deed, yet in desire.
WIIIT-SUNDAY.
Nay, startle not to hear that rushing
wind,
Wherewith this place is shaken:
   Attend a while, and thou shalt quick-
ly find,
How much thou art mistaken;
If thou think here

Is any cause of fear.

Scest thou not how on those twelve reverend heads
Sit cloven tongues of fire?
And as the rumour of that wonder spreads,
The multitude admire
To see it: and
Yet more amazed stand
To hear at once so great variety
Of language from them come,
Of whom they dare be bold to say they be
Bred no where but at home,
And never were
In place such words to hear.
Mock not, profane despisers of the Spirit,
At what's to you unknown:
This earnest he hath sent, who must inherit
All nations as his own:
That they may know
How much to him they owe.
Now that he is ascended up on high
To his celestial throne,
And hath led captive all captivity,
He'll not receive alone,
But likewise give
Gifts unto all that live;
To all that live by him, that they may be,
In his due time, each one,
Partakers with him in his victory,
Nor he triumph alone;
But take all his
Unto him where he is.
To fit them for which blessed state of glory,
This is his agent here:
To publish to the World that happy story,
Always, and every where,
This resident
Embassador is sent.
Heaven's liegcr upon earth to counter-work
The mines that Satan made,
And bring to light thoso enemies, that lurk
Under sin's gloomy shade:
That hell may not
Still boast what it hath got.
Thus Babel's curse, confusion, is retrieved; Diversity of tongues

By this division of the Spirit relieved:
And to prevent all wrongs, One faith unites
People of different rites.
0 let his entertainment then be such As doth him best befit:
Whatever he rcquircth think not much
Freely to yield him it:
For who doth this
Reaps the first-fruits of bliss.

TRINITY SUNDAY. GRACE, Wit, and Art, assist me; for I see
The subject of this day's solemnity
So far excels in worth,
That sooner may
I drain the sea,
Or drive the day With light away,
Than fully set it forth,
Except you join all three to take my part,
And chiefly Grace fill both my head and heart.
Stay, busy soul, presume not to enquire
Too much of what Angels can but admire,
And never comprehend:
The Trinity
Iu Unity,
And Unity
In Trinity, All reason doth transcend.
God Father, Son God, and God Holy Ghost, Who most admircth, magnifieth most.
And who most magnifies best understands,
And best cxpresscth what the heads, and hands,
And hearts, of all men living,
When most they try
To glorify,
And raise on high,
Fall short, and lie,
Grovelling below: Man's giving
Is but restoring by retail, with loss,
What from his God ho first received in gross.
Faith must perform the office of invention,
And Elocution, struck with apprehension
Of wonder, silence keep.
Not tongues, but eyes
Lift to the skies
In reverend wise, Best solemnize

This day: whereof the deep
Mysterious subject lies out of the reach
Of wit to learn, much more of Art to teach.
Then write *non Ultra* here; Look not for leave
To speak of what thou never canst conccivo
Worthily, as thou shouldst:
And it shall be
Enough for thee,
If none but he
Himself doth see, Though thou canst not, thou wouldst Make his praise glorious, who is alone Thrice blessed one in three, and three in one.

INVITATION.
Turn in, my Lord, turn in to me; Mine heart's a homely place;
But thou canst make corruption flee,
And fill it with thy grace:
So furnished it will be brave,
And a rich dwelling thou shalt have.
It was thy lodging once before,
It buildcd was by thee: But I to sin set ope the door,
It rendcr'd was by me. And so thy building was defaced, And in thy room another placed.
But he usurps, the right is thine: 0 dispossess him, Lord.
Do thou but say, This heart is mine,
He's gone at the first word.
Thy word's thy will, thy will's thy power,
Thy time is always; now's mine hour.
Now say to sin, depart:
And, *Son, give me thine heart.*
Thou, that by saying, *Let it be,* didst make it,
Canst, if thou wilt, by saying, *Give't me,* take it.

COMFORT IN EXTREMITY.
Alas! my Lord is going,
Oh my woe I
It will be mine undoing; If he go,
I'll run and overtake him:
If he stay,
I'll cry aloud, and make him
Look this way.
0 stay, my Lord, my Love, 'tis I;
Comfort me quickly, or I die.
Cheer up thy drooping spirits, I am here.
Mine all-svjficicnt merits

Shall appear
Before the throne of glory
In thy stead:
I'll put into thy story
What I did,
Lift up thine eyes, sad soul, and see
Thy Saviour here. Lo, I am he.

Alas! shall I present My sinfulness
To thee *I* thou wilt resent
The loathsomeness.
Be not afraid, I'll take
Thy Sins on me,
And all my favour make
To shine on thee.

Lord, what thou'lt havo rae, thou
must mate me. *As I have made thee now,*
I take thee. RESOLUTION AND ASSURAN-
CE.

Lord, thou wilt love me. Wilt thou
not?
Beshrcw that not:
It was my siu begot
That Question first: Yes, Lord, thou
wilt:
Thy blood was spilt
To wash away my guilt,
Lord, I will love thee. Shall I not?
Beshrew that not.
'Twas death's accursed plot
To put that question; Yes, I will,
Lord, love thee still,
In spite of all my ill.
Then life, and love continue still
Wc shall, and will,
My Lord and I, until,
In his celestial hill,
Wc love our fill,
When he hath purged all mine ilL
VOWS BROKEN AND RENEWED.

Said I not so, that I would sin no more
1
Witness my God, I did:
Yet I am run again upon the score:
My faults cannot be hid.
What shall I do? Make vows, and
break them still?
'Twill be but labour lost?
My good cannot prevail against mine
ill:
The business will be crost.
0, say not so: thou canst not tell what
strength
Thy God may give thee at the length:
Renew thy vows, and if thou keep the
last, Thy God will pardon all that's past.

Vow, whilst thou canst; whilo thou
canst vow, thou may'st
Perhaps perform it, when thou thinkest
least.
Thy God hath not denied thco all,
Whilst he permits thee but to call:
Call to thy God for grace to keep
Thy vows; and if thou break them,
weep.
Weep for thy broken vows, and vow
again:
Vows made with tears cannot be still in
vain.
Then once again
I vow to mend my ways;
Lord, say Amen,
And thine be all the praise.
CONFUSION.

0 How my mind Is gravell'd I
Not a thought,
That I can find,
But's ravcll'd
All to nought.
Short ends of threads,
And narrow shreds
  Of lists, Knot snarled ruffs,
  Loose broken tufts
  Of twists, Arc my torn meditation's
ragged clothing, Which, wound and wo-
ven shape a suit for nothing: One while
I think, and then I am in pain To think
how to unthink that thought again.
  How can my soul
  But famish
  With this food? Pleasure's full bowl
Tastes ramish, Taints the blood.
Profit picks bones,
  And chews on stones That choke:
Honour climbs hills,
  Fats not, but fills With smoke. And
whilst my thoughts arc greedy upon
these, They pass by pearls, and stoop to
pick up pease. Such wash and draff is fit
for none but swine: And such I am not,
Lord, if I am thine. Clothe me anew, and
feed me then afresh; Else my soul dies
famish'd, and starved with flesh.
Lints,' ' snarled rud",' &c.: oM pieces
of dress.—' ' Kamish:' what is called in
Scotland ' wcrsh,' i. c, taotclcss.
A PARADOX.
THE WORSE THE BETTER.
Welcome mine health: this sickness
makes me well.
  Medicines adieu: When with diseases

I have list to dwell,
  I'll wish for you.
  Weleome my strength: this weakness
makes me able.
Powers adieu:
When I am weary grown of standing
stable,
  I'll wish for you.
  Weleome my wealth: this loss hath
gain'd me more.
Riches adieu:
When I again grow greedy to bo poor,
  I'll wish for you.
  Weleome my credit: this disgrace is
glory.
Honours adieu:
When for renown and fame I shall be
sorry,
  I'll wish for you.
  Weleome content: this sorrow is my
joy.
Pleasures adieu:
When I desiro such griefs as may an-
noy,
  I'll wish for you.
  Health, strength, and riches, credit,
and content,
Are spared best, sometimes, when they
are spent:
Sickness and weakness, loss, disgrace,
and sorrow,
Lend most sometimes, when they seem
most to borrow.
  Blest bo that hand, that helps by hurt-
ing, gives
  By taking, by forsaking me relieves.
  If in my fall my rising be thy will,
  Lord, I will say, *The worse the better*
still.
  I'll speak the Paradox, maintain thou
it,
  And let thy grace supply my want of
wit
  Leave me no learning that a man may
see,
  So I may be a scholar unto thee.
INMATES.
A House I had (a heart, I mean), so
wide,
  And full of spacious rooms on every
side,
That viewing it I thought I might do
well,
  Rather than keep it void, and make no
gain,

Of what I could not use, to entertain
Such guests as came: I did; But what befell
Me quickly in that course, I sigh to tell.
A guest I had (alas! I have her still),
A great big bellied guest, enough to fill
The vast content of hell, Corruption.
By entertaining her, I lost my right
To more than all the world hath now in sight.
Each day, each hour, almost, she brought forth one,
Or other base begot Transgression.
The charge grew great. I, that had lost before
All that I had, was forced now to score
For all the charges of their maintenance
In dooms-day book: Whoever knew't would say
The least sum there was more than I could pay,
When first 'twas due, besides continuance,
Which could not choose but much the debt enhance,
s
To case me first I wish'd her to remove:
But she would not. I sued her then above,
And begg'd the Court of heaven but in vain
To cast her out. No, I could not evade
The bargain, which she pleaded I had made,
That, whilst both lived, I should entertain,
At mine own charge, both her and all her train.
No help then, but or I must die or she;
And yet my death of no avail would be:
For one death I had died already then,
When first she lived in me: and now to die
Another death agaiu were but to tie,
And tM'ist them both into a third, which when It once hath seized on, never looseth men.
Her death might be my life; but her to kill
I, of myself, had neither power nor will.
So desperate was my case. Whilst I

delay'd,
My guest still teem'd, my debts still greater grew;
The less I had to pay, the more was due.
The more I knew, the more I was afraid:
The more I mused, the more I was dismay'd.
At last I learn'd, there was no way but one:
A friend must do it for me. He alone,
That is the Lord of life, by dying can
Save men from death, and kill Corruption:
And many years ago the deed was done,
His heart was pierced; out of his side there ran
Sins' corrosives, restoratives for man.
This precious balm I begg'd, for pity's sake,
At Mercy's gate: where Faith alone may take
What Grace and Truth do offer liberally.
Bounty said, Come. I heard it, and believed;
None ever there complain'd but was relieved.
Hope waiting upon Faith said instantly,
That thenceforth I should live, Corruption die.
And so she died, I live. But yet, alas!
We are not parted: She is where she was,
Cleaves fast unto me still, looks through mine eyes,
Speaks in my tongue, and museth in my mind,
Works with mine hands: her body 's left behind,
Although her soul be gone. My miseries
All flow from hence; from hence my woes arise.
I loathe myself, because I leave her not;
Yet cannot leave her. No, she is my lot,
Now being dead, that living was my choice;
And still, though dead, she both conceives and bears,
Many faults daily, and as many fears:
All which for vengeance call with a loud voice,
And drown my comforts with their

deadly noise.
Dead bodies kept unburied quickly stink
And putrefy. How can I then but think
Corruption noisome, even mortified?
Though such she were before, yet such to me
She seemed not. Kind fools can never see,
Or will not credit, until they have tried,
That friendly looks oft false intents do hide.
But mortified Corruption lies unmask'd,
Blabs her own secret filthiness unask'd,
To all that understand her. That do none
In whom she lives embraced with delight:
She first of all deprives them of their sight;
Then dote they on her, as upon their own,
And she to them seems beautiful alone.
But woe is me! One part of me is dead;
The other lives: Yet that which lives is led,
Or rather carried captive unto sin,
By the dead part. I am a living grave,
And a dead body I within me have.
The worse part of the better, oft doth win:
And, when I should have ended, I begin.
Tho scent would choke me, were it not that graco
Sometimes vouchsafeth to perfume the place
With odours of the Spirit, which do case me, And counterpoise Corruption.
Blessed Spirit, Although eternal torments be my merit,
And of myself Transgressions only please me,
Add grace enough being revived to raise me.
Challenge thine own. Let not intruders hold
Against thy right, what to my wrong I sold.
Having no state myself, but tenancy,
And tenancy at will, what could I grant
That is not voided, if thou say, Avaunt!
0 speak the word, and make these inmates flee Or, which is one, take me to

dwell with thee.

THE CURB.

Peace, rebel thought: dost thou not
know thy King, My God, is here *l*
Cannot his presence, if no other thing,
Make thee forbear *l*
Or were he absent, all the standers by
Are but his spies:
And well he knows, if thou shouldst it
deny,
Thy words were lies.
If others will not, yet I must, and will,
  Myself complain.
  My God, even now a base rebellious
thought Began to move,
And subt'ly twining with me would
have wrought
Me from thy love:
Fain he would have me to believe, that
Sin
And thou might both
Take up my heart together for your Inn,
And neither loathe
The other's company: a while sit still,
  And part again.
  Tell me, my God, how this may be re-
drest: The fault is great,
And I the guilty party have confest,
I must be beat.
And I refuse not punishment for this,
Though to my pain;
So I may learn to do no more amiss,
  Nor sin again:
  Correct me, if thou wilt; but teach me
then, What I shall do.
  Lord of my life, methinks I heard
thee say.
That labour's eased:
The fault, that is confess'd, is done
away,
And thou art pleased.
How can I sin again, and wrong thee
then,
That dost relent,
And cease thine anger straight, as soon
as men
Do but repent?
No, rebel thought; for if thou move
again,
I'll tell that too.

TUB LOSS.

The match is made Between my Love
and me:
And therefore glad
And merry now I'll be.

Come, glory, crown
My head;
And, pleasures, drown
My bed
Of thorns in down.
Sorrow, be gone;
Delight
And joy alone
Befit
My honey-moon.
Be packing now,
  You cumb'rous cares, and fears
Mirth will allow No room to sighs and
tears.
Whilst thus I lay,
As ravish'd with delight,
I heard one say,
So fools their friends requite.
I knew the voice,
  My Lord's,
  And at the noise
His words Did make, arose.
I look'd, and spied
  Each where,
  And loudly cried,
  My dear; But none replied:
Then to my grief
I found my Love was gone,
Without relief,
  Leaving me all alone.

THE SEARCH.

Whither, oh! whither is my Lord de-
parted *l* What can my Love, that is so
tender-hearted, Forsake the soul, which
once he thorough darted, As if it never
smarted?
  No, sure my Love is here, if I could
find him: He that fills all can leave no
place behind him. But oh! my senses are
too weak to wind him: Or else I do not
mind him.
O no, I mind him not so as I ought;
Nor seek him so as I by him was sought,
When I had lost myself: he dearly
bought
Me, that was sold for nought.
But I have wounded him, that made me
sound;
Lost him again, by whom I first was
found:
Him, that exalted me, have cast to the
ground;
My sins his blood have drowu'd.
Tell me, oh J tell me (thou alone canst
tell),

Lord of my life, where thou art gone to
dwell:
. For, in thy absence heaven itself is
hell:
Without thee none is well.
  Or, if thou beest not gone, but only
hidest
Thy presence in the place where thou
abidest,
Teach me the sacred art, which thou
providest
  For all them, whom thou guidest,
  To seek and find thee by. Else here
I'll lie,
Until thou find me. If thou let me die,
That only unto thee for life do cry,
  Thou diest as well as I.
  For, if thou live in me, and I in thee,
Then either both alive, or dead must be:
At least I'll lay my death on thee, and
see
If thou wilt not agree.
  For, though thou be the Judge thyself,
I have
Thy promise for it, which thou canst not
wave,
That who salvation at thine hands do
crave,
Thou wilt not fail to save.
  Oh! seek, and find me then; or else
deny
Thy truth, thyself. Oh! thou that canst
not lie,
Show thyself constant to thy word, draw
nigh.
Find me. Lo, here I lie.

THE RETURN.

  Lo, now my Love appears;
  My tears Have clear'd mine eyes: I
see 'Tis he. Thanks, blessed Lord, thine
absence was my hell; And, now thou art
returned, I am well.
  By this I see I must
  Not trust My joys unto myself: This
shelf, Of too secure, and too presumptu-
ous pleasure, Had almost sunk my ship,
and drown'd my treasure.
  "Who would have thought a joy So
coy
To be oiFended so,
And go
So suddenly away? As if enjoying
Full pleasure and contentment, were an-
noying.
  Hereafter I had need Take heed.

Joys, amongst other things,
. Have wings,
    And watch their opportunities of flight,
Converting in a moment day to night.
    But, is't enough for mo To be
Instructed to bo wise?
I'll rise,
And read a lecture unto them that aro
Willing to learn, how comfort dwells with caro.
    He that his joys would keep
    Must weep; And in the brine of tears
And fears Must pickle them. That powder will preserve: Faith with repentanco is the soul's conserve.
    Learn to make much of care:
    A rare And precious balsam 'tis For bliss; Which oft resides, where mirth with sorrow meets; Heavenly joys on earth arc bitter-sweets.

INUNDATIONS.

We talk of *Noah's* flood, as of a wonder;
And well we may;
The Scriptures say,
The water did prevail, the hills were under,
And nothing could be Been but sea.
    And yet there arc two other floods surpass
    That Hood, as far,
    As heaven one star, Which many men regard, as little, as The ordinariest tilings that are.
    The one is Sin, the other is Salvation:
    And vc must need Confess indeed,
That cither of them is an inundation,
Which doth the deluge far exceed.
    In Noah's flood he and his household lived:
    And there abodc
    A whole Ark-load Of other creatures, that were then reprieved: All safely on the waters rode.
    But when Sin came, it overflowed all,
    And left none free:
    Nay, even he, That knew no sin, could not release my thrall, But that he was made sin for me;
    And, when Salvation came, my Saviour's blood
    Drown'd Sin again, With all its train Of evils, overflowing them with good, With good that ever shall remain.
0, let there bo one other inundation,

Let Grace o'crilow In my soul so,
That thankfulness may level with Salvation,
And sorrow Sin may overgrow.
    Then will I praise my Lord and Saviour 80,
    That Angels shall
    Admire man's fall,
    When they shall see God's greatest glory grow,
Where Satan thought to root out all.

SIN.

    Sin, I would fain define thee; but thou art
    An uncouth thing: All that I bring
To show thee fully, shows thee but in part.
    I call thec the transgression of the Law,
    And yet I read
That Sin is dead Without the Law; and thence its strength doth draw.
    I say thou art the sting of death. Tis true:
    And yet I find
    Death comes behind: The work is done before the pay bo due.
    I say thou art the devil's work; Yet ho
    Should much rather Call thee father;
For ho had been no devil but for thee.
    What shall I call thee then / If death and devil,
    Right understood, Be names too good,
I'll say thou art the quintessence of evil.

TRAVELS AT HOME.

    Oft have I wish'd a traveller to be:
Mine eyes did even itch the sights to see,
That I had heard and read of. Oft I have llccn greedy of occasion, as the grave,
That never says, enough; yet still was crost,
When opportunities had promised most.
At last l said, What mcan'st thou, wandering elf,
To straggle thus? Go travel first thyself.
Thy little world can show thee wonders great:
    The greater may have more, but not more neat
And curious pieces..Search, and thou shalt find
Enough to talk of. If thou wilt, thy mind Europe supplies, and Asia thy will,

And Afric thine affections. And if still
Thou list to travel further, put thy senses
For both the Indies. Make no more pretences
Of new discoveries, whilst yet thine own,
And nearest, little world is still unknown.
Away then with thy quadrants, compasses,
Globes, tables, cards, and maps, and minute glasses;
Lay by thy journals, and thy diaries,
Close up thine annals, and thine histories.
Study thyself, and read what thou hast writ
In thine own book, thy conscience. Is it fit
To labour after other knowledge so,
And thine own nearest, dearest, self not know /
Travels abroad both dear and dangerous are,
Whilst oft the soul pays for the body's fare:
Travels at home are cheap, and safe.

Salvation

Comes mounted on the wings of meditation.
lie that doth live at home, and learns to know
God and himself, needeth no further go.

THE JOURNEY.

    Like is a journey. From our mothers' wombs,
    As houses, we set out: and in our tombs,
    As inns, we rest, till it be time to rise.
    Twixt rocks and gulfs our narrow foot-path lies:
    Haughty presumption and hell-deep despair
    Make our way dangerous, though seeming fair.
    The world, with its enticements sleek and sly,
    Slabbers our steps, and makes them slippery.
    The flesh, with its corruptions, clogs our feet,
    And burdens us with loads of lusts unmeet.
    The devil, where we tread, doth spread his snares,

And with temptations takes us unawares.

Our footsteps arc our thoughts, our
words, our works:

Theso carry us along; in these there
lurks

Envy, lust, avarice, ambition,

The crooked turnings to perdition.

One while we creep amongst the
thorny brakes

Of worldly profits; and the devil
takes

Delight to see us pierce ourselves
with sorrow

To-day, by thinking what may be to-
morrow.

Another while we wade, and wallow
in

Puddles of pleasure: and we never lin

Daubing ourselves, with dirty
damn'd delights,

Till self-begotten pain our pleasure
frights.

Sometimes we scramble to get up the
banks

Of icy honour; and we break our
ranks

To step before our fellows; though,
they say,

He soonest tircth, that still leads the
way.

' Lin:' cciuie.

Sometimes, when others justle and provoke us,

Wo stir that dust ourselves, that.ser-
vos to ehokc us;

And raise thosc tempests of contention, which

Blow us beside the way into the
ditch.

Our minds should be our guides; but
they arc blind:

Our wills outrun our wits, or lag behind.

Our furious passions, like unbridled
jades,

Hurry us headlong to tho infernal
shades.

If God be not our guide, our guard,
our friend.

Eternal death will be our journey's end.

ENGINES.

Men often find, when Nature's at a
stand,

And hath in vain tried all her utmost
strength,

That Art, her Ape, can reach her out a
hand.

To piece her powers with to a lull
length.

And may not Grace have means
enough in store

Wherewith to do as much as that, and
more?

She may: she hath engines of every
kind,

To work, what Art and Nature, when
they view,

Stupendous miracles of wonder find,

And yet must needs acknowledge to be
true;

So far transcending all their power and
might,

That they amazed stand even at the
sight.

Take but three instances; Faith,
Hope, and Love.

Souls help'd by the perspective glass
of Faith

Are able to perceive what is above

The reach of Reason: yea, the Scrip-
ture saith,

Even him that is invisible behold,

And future things, as if they'd been of
old.

Faith looks into the secret Cabinet

Of God's eternal Counsels, and doth
see

Such mysteries of glory there, as set

Believing hearts on longing, till they
be

Transform'd to the same image, and appear

So altered, as if themselves were there.

Faith can raise earth to heaven, or
draw down

Heaven to earth, make both extremes
to meet,

Felicity and misery, can crown

Reproach with honour, season sour
with sweet.

Nothing's impossible to Faith: a man

May do all things that he believes ho
can.

Hope founded upon Faith can raise
the heart

Above itself in expectation

Of what the soul desireth for its part:

Then, when its time of transmigration

Is dclay'd longest, yet as patiently

To wait, as if 'twere answer'd by and
by.

When grief unwieldy grows, Hope
can abate

The bulk to what proportion it will:

So that a large circumference of late

A little centre shall not reach to fill.

Nor that, which giant-like before did
strout,

Be able with a pigmy's pace to hold out.

Hope can disperse the thickest clouds
of night,

That fear hath overspread the soul
withal;

And make the darkest shadows shine
as bright

As the Sunbeams spread on a silver
wall.

Sin-shaken souls Hope anchor-like
holds steady,

When storm and tempests make them
more than giddy.

Love led bv Faith, and fed with Hope, is
able

To travel through the world's wide
wilderness;

And burdens seeming most intolerable

Both to take up, and bear with cheerfulness.

To do, or suller, what appears in sight

Extremely heavy, Love will make most
light.

'Strunt:' strut.

Yea, what by men is done, or suf-
fered,

Either for God, or else for one another,

Though in itself it be much blemished

With many imperfections, which
smother,

And drown, the worth, and weight of
it; yet, fall

What will, or can, Love makes amends
for all.

Love doth unite, and knit, both make,
and keep

Things one together, which were other-
wise,

Or would be both diverse, and distant.
Deep,

High, long, and broad, or whatsoever
size

Eternity is of, or happiness,

Love comprehends it all, be't more or
less.

Give me this threefold cord of graces then,

Faith, Hope, and Love, let them possess mine heart,

And gladly I'll resign to other men All I can claim by Nature or by Art.

To mount a soul, and make it still stand stable, These arc alone Engines incomparable.

JACULA PEUDENTUM; OR, OUTLANDISH PROVERBS, SENTENCES, ETC. SELECTED BY MR GEORGE HERBERT, LATE ORATOR OF THE UNIVERSITY OF CAMBRIDGE. JACULA PRUDENTUM.

Old men go to Death, Death comes to young men.

!Man proposcth, God disposcth. lie begins to die, that quits his desires.

A handful of good life is better than a bushel of Learning.

lie that studios his content, wants it.

Every day brings its bread with it.

Humble hearts have humble desires.

He that stumbles and falls not, mends his pace

The house shows the owner.

lie that gets out of debt, grows rich.

All is well with him who is beloved of his neighbours.

Building and marrying of Children arc great wasters.

A good bargain is a pick-purse.

The scalded dog fears cold water.

Pleasing ware is half sold.

Light burdens, long borne, grow heavy.

The Wolf knows what the ill beast thinks.

"Who hath none to still him, may weep out his eyes.

"When all sins grow old, covetousness is young.

If ye would know a knave, give him a staff.

You cannot know wine by the barrel.

A cool mouth, and warm feet, live long.

A horse made, and a man to make.

Look not for musk in a dog's kcunci.

Not a long lay, but a good heart, rids work.

He pulls with a long rope, that waits for another's death.

Great strokes make not sweet music.

A cask and an ill custom must be broken.

A fat housekeeper makes lean executors.

Empty chambers make foolish maids.

The gentle Hawk half mans herself.

The Devil is not always at one door.

When a friend asks, there is no tomorrow.

God sends cold according to clothes.

One sound blow will serve to undo us all.

lie loscth nothing, that loscth not God.

The German's wit is in his fingers.

At dinner my man appears.

Who gives to all, denies all.

Quick believers need broad shoulders.

Who remove stones, bruise their fingers.

Benefits please like flowers while they are fresh.

Between the business of life and the day of death, a spaco ought to be interposed. All came from and will go to others. He that will take the bird, must not scare it. He lives unsafely that looks too near on things. A gentle housewife mars the household. A crooked log makes a straight fire. He hath great need of a fool that plays the fool himself. A Merchant that gains not, loscth. Let not him that fears feathers come among wild-fowl. Love, and a Cough, cannot be hid. A Dwarf on a Giant's shoulder sees further of the two. lie that sends a fool, means to follow him. Brabbling Curs never want sore ears. Better the feet slip than the tongue. For washing his hands, none sells his lands.

A Lion's skin is never cheap.

The goat must browse where she is tied.

Nothing is to be presumed on, or despaired of.

Who hath a Wolf for his mate, needs a Dog for his man.

In a good house all is quickly ready.

A bad dog never sees the Wolf.

God oft hath a great share in a little house.

Ill ware is never cheap.

A cheerful look makes a dish a feast.

If all fools had baubles, we should want fuel.

Virtue never grows old.

Evening words are not like to morning.

Were there no fools, bad ware would not pass.

Never had ill workman good tools.

He stands not surely that never slips.

Were there no hearers, there would be no backbiters.

Every thing is of use to a housekeeper.

When prayers are done, my Lady is ready.

Cities seldom change Religion only.

At length the Fox turns Monk.

Flies are busiest about lean horses.

Hearken to reason, or she will be heard.

The bird loves her nest.

Every thing new is fine.

When a dog is a drowning, every one offers him drink.

Better a bare foot than none.

Who is so deaf as he that will not hear?

lie that is warm thinks all so.

At length the Fox is brought to the Furrier.

He that goes bare-foot must not plant thorns.

They that aro booted are not always ready.

Ho that will learn to pray, let him go to Sea.

In spending lies the advantage.

He that lives well, is learned enough.

Ill vessels seldom miscarry.

A full belly neither fights nor flies well.

All truths arc not to be told.

An old wise man's shadow is better than a young buzzard's

Noble housekeepers need no doors. sword.

Every ill man hath his ill day.

Sleep without supping, and wake without owing.

I gave the mouse a hole, and she is become my heir.

Assail who will, the valiant attends.

Whither goest, grief? where I am wont.

Praise day at night, and life at the end.

Whither shall the Ox go where he shall not labour?

Where you think there is bacon, there

is no chimney.

Mend your clothes, and you may hold out this year.

Tress a stick, and it seems a youth.

The tongue walks where the teeth speed not.

A fair wife and a frontier Castle breed quarrels.

Leave jesting whiles it pleaseth, lest it turn to earnest.

Deceive not thy Physician, Confessor, nor Lawyer.

Ill natures, the more you ask them, the more they stick.

Virtue and a Trade are the best portion for children.

The Chicken is the Country's, but the City eats it.

He that gives thee a Capon, give him the leg and the wing.

lie that lives ill, fear follows him.

Give a clown your finger, and he will take your hand.

Good is to be sought out, and evil attended.

A good paymaster starts not at assurances.

Xo Alchymy to saving.

To a grateful man give money when he asks.

Who would do ill ne'er wants occasion.

To fine folks a little ill finely wrapt.

To a fair day, open the window, but make you ready as to

A child correct behind, and not before. a foul.

Keep good men company, and you shall be of the number.

No lovo to a Father's.

The Mill gets by going.

To a boiling pot flies come not.

Make haste to an ill way, that you may get out of it.

A snow year, a rich year.

Better to be blind than to sec ill.

Learn weeping, and thou shalt laugh gaining.

Who hath no more bread than need, must not keep a dog.

A garden must be looked unto, and dressed as the body.

The Fox, when he cannot reach the grapes, says, They arc

AVatcr trotted is as good as oats. not

ripe.

Though the Mastiff be gentle, yet bite him not by the lip."

Though a lio be well drest, it is ever overcome.

Though old and wise, yet still advise.

Three helping one another, bear the burthen of six.

Slander is a shipwreck by a dry Tempest.

Old wine and an old friend arc good provisions.

Happy is he that chastens himself.

Well may he smell fire, whose gown bums.

The wrongs of a Husband or Master are not reproached.

Welcome evil, if thou comest alone.

Love your neighbour, yet pull not down your hedge.

The bit that one cats, no friend makes.

A drunkard's purse is a bottle.

She spins well that breeds her children.

Play with a fool at home, and he will play with you in the

Good is the *mora* that makes all sure. market.

Every one stretcheth his legs according to his coverlet.

Autumnal Agues are long or mortal.

Marry your son when you Mill; your daughter when you can-

Dally not with money or women.

Men speak of the Fair as things went with them there.

The best remedy against an ill man, is much ground between

The mill cannot grind with water that's past. both

Corn is cleaned with wind, and the soul with chastenings,

Good words arc worth much, and cost little.

To buy dear is not bounty.

Jest not with the eye, or with Religion.

The eye and Religion can bear no jesting.

Without favour none will know you, and with it you will not

Buy at a fair, but sell at home. know yourself.

Cover yourself with your shield, and care not for cries.

A wicked man's gift hath a touch of

his master.!

None is a fool always, every one sometimes.

From a choleric man, withdraw a little; from him that says

Debtors arc liars. nothing, for ever.

Of all smells, bread: of all tastes, salt.

In a great River great fish are found: but take heed lest vou be drowned.

Ever since we wear clothes, we know not one another.

God heals, and the Physician hath the thanks.

I fell is full of good meanings and wishings.

Take heed of still waters, the quick pass away.

After the house is finished, leave it.

Our own actions are our security, not others' judgments.

Think of ease, but work on.

lie that lies long abed, his estate feels it.

Whether you boil snow or pound it, you can have but water

One stroke fells not an oak. of it.

God complains not, but doth what is fitting.

A diligent Scholar, and the Master's paid.

Milk says to wine, Weleome, friend.

They that know one another, salute afar off.

Where there is no honour, there is no grief.

Where the drink goes in, there the wit goes out

He that stays, does the business.

Alms never make poor. Or thus,

Great alms-giving lessens no man's living.

Giving much to the poor, doth enrich a man's store.

It takes much from the account, to which his sin doth amount.

It adds to the glory both of soul and body.

Ill comes in by ells, and goes out by inches.

The smith and his penny both arc black.

"Whoso house is of glass, must not throw stones at another.

If the old dog bark, he gives counsel.

The tree that grows slowly, keeps itself for another.

I wept when I was born, and every day shows why.

lie that looks not before, finds himself behind.

He that plays his money, ought not to value it.

He that riscth first, is first drest.

Diseases of the eye arc to bo cured with the elbow.

A gentleman's greyhound and a salt-box, seek them at the

The hole calls the thief. fire.

A child's service is little, yet he is no little fool that de

The river past, and God forgotten. spiscth it.

Evils have their comfort; good none can support (to wit) with a moderate and contented heart.

Who must account for himself and others, must know both.

He that eats the hard, shall cat the ripe.

The miserable man makcth a penny of a farthing, and the

liberal of a farthing sixpence.

The honey is sweet, but the Bee stings.

Weight and measure take away strife.

The son full and tattered, the daughter empty and fine.

Every path hath a puddle.

In good years corn is hay, in ill years straw is corn.

Send a wise man on an errand, and say nothing unto him.

In life you loved me not, in death you bewail me.

Into a mouth shut flies fly not.

Tie heart's letter is read in the eyes.

The ill that comes out of our mouth falls into our bosom.

In great pedigrees there are Governors and Chandlers.

In thc house of a fiddler, all fiddle.

Sometimes the best gain is to lose.

Working and making a fire doth discretion require.

One grain fills not a sack, but helps his fellows.

It is a great victory that comes without blood.

In war, hunting, and love, men for one pleasure a thousand

Truth and oil are ever above. griefs prove.

Reckon right, and February hath one-and-thirty days.

Honour without profit is a ring on the finger.

Estate in two Parishes is bread in two wallets.

Honour and profit lie not in one sack.

A naughty child is better sick than whole.

lie that riscth betimes, hath something in his head.

Advise none to Marry or go to war.

To steal the Hog, and give the feet for alms.

The thorn comes forth with the point forwards.

One hand washcth another, and both the face.

The fault of the horse is put on the saddle.

The corn hides itself in the snow as an old man in furs.

The Jews spend at Easter, the Moors at marriages, the

Punishment is lame, but it comes. Christians iu suits.

Fine dressing is a foul house swept before the doors.

A woman and a glass are ever in danger.

An ill wound is cured, not an ill name.

The wise hand doth not all that the foolish mouth speaks.

On painting and fighting look aloof.

Knowledge is folly, except grace guide it.

The more women look in their glass, the less they look to

A long tongue is a sign of a short hand. their house.

Marry a widow before she leave mourning.

The worst of law is, that one suit breeds twenty.

Providence is better than a rent.

What your glass tells you, will not be told by Counsel.

There are more men threatened than stricken.

A fool knows more in his house, than a wise man in another's.

I had rather ride on an ass that carries me, than a horse

that throws me.

The hard gives more than he that hath nothing.

The beast that goes always, never wants blows.

Good cheap is dear.

It costs more to do ill than to do well.

Good words quench more than a bucket of water.

An ill agreement is better than a good judgment.

There is more talk than trouble.

Better spare to have of thine own, than ask of other men.

Better good afar off, than evil at hand.

Fear keeps the garden better than the gardener.

I had rather ask of my fire brown bread, than borrow of my

neighbour white.

Your pot broken seems better than my whole one.

Let an ill man lie in thy straw, and he looks to be thy heir.

By suppers more have been killed than *Galen* ever cured.

"While the discreet advise, the fool doth his business.

A mountain and a river arc good neighbours.

Gossips arc frogs, they drink and talk.

Much spends the traveller more than the abidcr.

Prayers and provender hinder no journey.

A well-bred youth neither speaks of himself, nor, being spoken to, is silent.

A journeying woman speaks much of all, and all of her.

The Fox knows much, but more he that catchcth him.

Many friends in general, one in special.

The fool asks much, but he is more fool that grants it.

Many kiss the hand they wish cut off.

Neither bribe, nor lose thy right.

In the world who knows not to swim, goes to the bottom.

Choose not a house near an Inn (viz. for noise); or in a corner (for filth).

lie is a fool that thinks not that another thinks.

Neither eyes on letters, nor hands in coffers.

The lion is not so fierce as they paint him.

Go not for every grief to the Physician, nor for every quarrel to the Lawyer, nor for every thirst to the pot. Good service is a great enchantment. There would be no great ones, if there were no little oues. It is no sure rule to fish with a cross-bow. There were no ill language, if it were not ill taken. The groundsel speaks not, save what it heard at the hinges. The best mirror is an old friend. Say no ill of the year till it be past. A man's discontent is his worst evil. Fear nothing but sin.

The child says nothing, but what it heard by the fire. Call me not an olive, till thou see me gathered. That is not good language which all understand not. He that burns his house, warms himself for once, He will burn his house to warm his hands. He will spend a whole year's rent at one meal's meat. All is not gold that ''listers. A blustering night, a fair day. Be not idle, and you shall not be longing. He is not poor that hath little, but he that desireth much. Let none say, I will not drink water.

He wrongs not an old man that steals his supper from him.

The tongue talks at the head's cost.

He that strikes with his tongue, must ward with his head.

Keep not ill men company, lest you increase the number.

God strikes not with both hands, for to the sea he wade

heavens, and to rivers fords.

A rugged stone grows smooth from hand to hand.

No lock will hold against the power of gold.

The absent party is still faulty.

Peace and patience, and death with repentance

If you lose your time, you cannot get money nor gain.

Be not a Baker, if your head be of butter.

Ask much to have a little.

Little sticks kindle the fire; great ones put it out.

Another's bread costs dear.

Although it rain, throw not away thy watering pot.

Although the sun shine, leave not thy cloak at home.

A little with quiet is the only diet.

In vain is the mill-clack, if the Miller his hearing lack.

By the needle you shall draw the thread, and by that which is past, see how that which is to come will be drawn on. Stay a little, and news will find you. Stay till tho lame messenger come, if you will know the truth of the thing. When God will, no wind but brings rain. Though you rise early, yet the day comes at his time, and Pull down your hat on the wind's side. not till then.

As the year is, your pot must seethe. Since you know all, and I nothing, tell me what I dreamed When the Fox preachcth, beware geese. last night.

"When you arc an Anvil, hold you still; when you arc a He that sows, trusts in God. hammer, strike your fill.

lie that makes his bed ill, lies there.

lie that labours and thrives, spins gold.

Poor and liberal, rich and covetous.

He that lies with the dogs, riscth with fleas.

lie that repairs not a part, builds all.

A discontented man knows not where to sit easy.

Who spits against heaven, it falls in his face.

lie that dines and leaves, lays the cloth twice.

Who cats his cock alone, must saddle his horse alone.

Ho that doth what he will, doth not what ho ought.

He that will deceive tbe Fox must rise betimes.

Ho that is not handsome at twenty, nor strong at thirty, nor rich at forty, nor wise at fifty, will never be handsome, strong, rich, or wise.

He that lives well, sees afar off.

lie that hath a mouth of his own, must not say to another,

He that will be served, must be patient. Blow.

lie that gives thee a bone, would not have thee die. lie that chastens one, chastens twenty. 1 Ic that hath lost his credit, is dead to the world.

He that hath no ill fortune, is troubled with good.

lie that demands, misscth not, unless his demands be foolish.

Ho that hath no honey in his pot, let him have it in his lie that takes not up a pin, slights his wife. mouth.

lie that owes nothing, if he makes not mouths at us, is

He that loseth his due, gets not thanks. courteous.

lie that believes all, misscth; he that belicveth nothing, hits

A married man turns his staff into a stake. not.

Pardons and pleasantness arc great revenges of slanders.

If you would know secrets, look them in grief or pleasure.

Serve a noble disposition; though poor, the time comes that he will repay thee.

The fault is as great as he that is faulty.

If folly were grief, every house would weep.

Ho that would be well old, must be old betimes.

Sit in your place, and none can make you rise.

If you could run as you drink, you might catch a hare.

Would you know what money is, Go borrow some.

The morning Sun never lasts a day.

Thou hast death in thy house, and dost bewail another's.

All griefs with bread arc less.

All things require skill but an appetite.

All things have their place, knew we how to place them.

Little pitchers have wide cars.

Wo arc fools one to another.

This world is nothing except it tend to another.

There are three ways, the Universities, the Sea, the Court.

God comes to sec without a bell.

Life without a friend, is death without a witness.

Clothe thee in war, arm thee in peace.

The horse thinks one thing, and he that saddles him another.

Wills and wives ever want.

The dog that licks ashes, trust not

with meal.

The buyer needs a hundred eyes, the seller not one.

He carries well, to whom it weighs not.

The comforter's head never aches.

Step.after step the ladder is ascended.

Who likes not the drink, God deprives him of bread.

To a crazy ship all winds are contrary.

Justice pleascth few in their own houso.

In time comes he, whom God sends.

Water afar oft" quencheth not fire.

In sports and journeys men are known.

An old friend is a new house.

Love is not found in the market.

Dry feet, warm head, bring safe to bed.

lie is rich enough that wants nothing.

One father is enough to govern ouo hundred sons, but not a hundred sons one father. Far shooting never killed bird. An upbraided morsel never choked any. Dearths foreseen come not. An ill labourer quarrels with his tools. He that falls into the dirt, the longer he stays there the 1 Ic that blames, would buy. fouler he is.

lie that sings on Friday, will weep on Sunday. The charges of building, and making of gardens arc unknown. My house, my house, though thou art small, thou art to mo the Escurial.

A hundred load of thought will not pay one of debts.

lie that comes of a hen must scrape.

He that seeks trouble never misses.

Being on sea, sail; being on land, settle.

Who doth his own business, fouls not his hands.

He that makes a good war, makes a good peace.

lie that works after his own manner, his head aches not at lie that once deceives, is ever suspected. the matter

"Who hath bitter in his mouth, spits not all sweet.

He that hath children, all his morsels are not his own.

He that hath the spice, may season as ho list.

He that hath a head of wax, must not walk in the sun.

lie that hath love in his breast, hath spurs in his sides. lie that hath a fox for his mate, hath need of a net at his

He that respects not, is not respected. girdle.

lie that hath right, fears; he that hath wrong, hopes.

He that hath patience, hath fat thrushes for a farthing.

Never was strumpet fair.

He that measures not himself is measured.

He that hath one hog, makes him fat; and he that hath one son, makes him a fool. Who lets his Wife go to every feast, and his horse drink at every water, shall neither have good wife nor good horse. He that speaks sows, and he that holds his peace gathers, lie that hath little is the less dirty. He that lives most dies most.

lie that hath one foot in the straw hath another in the spittle. He that is fed at another's hand, may stay long ere he be He that makes a thing too fine, breaks it. full.

He that bewails himself hath the cure in his hands.

He that would be well, needs not go from his own house.

Counsel breaks not the head.

Fly the pleasure that bites to-morrow.

Ho that knows what may bo gained in a day, never steals.

u

Money refused loseth its brightness.

Health and money go far.

Where your will is ready, your feet arc light.

A great ship asks deep waters.

Woe to the house where there is no chiding.

Take heed of the vinegar of sweet wine.

Fools bite one another, but wise men agree together.

Trust not one night's ice.

Good is good, but better carries it.

To gain teachcth how to spend.

Good finds good.

The dog gnaws the bone because he cannot swallow it.

The crow bewails the sheep, and then

eats it.

Building is a sweet impoverishing.

The first degree of folly is to hold one's self wise, the second to profess it, the third to despise counsel. The greatest step is that out of doors. To weep for joy is a kind of Manna. The first service a child doth his father is to make him foolish. The resolved mind hath no cares. In the kingdom of a cheater, the wallet is carried before. The eye will have his part. The good mother says not, Will you? but gives. A house and a woman suit excellently. In the kingdom of blind men, the one eyed is king. A little Kitchen makes a large house. War makes thieves, and peace hangs them. Poverty is the mother of health. In the morning mountains, in the evening fountains. The back door robs the house. Wealth is like rheum, it falls on the weakest parts. The gown is his that wears it, and the world his that enjoys Hope is the poor man's bread. it.

Virtue now is in herbs, and stones, and words only.

Fiuc words dress ill deeds.

Labour as long-lived, pray as even dying.

A poor beauty finds more lovers than husbands.

Discreet women have neither eyes nor cars.

Things well fitted abide.

Prcttiness dies first.

Talking pays no toll.

The master's eye fattens the horse, and his foot the ground.

Disgraces arc like cherries, one draws another.

Praise a hill, but keep below.

Praise the sea, but keep on land.

In choosing a wife, and buying a sword, wc ought not to

The wearer knows where the shoe wrings. trust another.

Fair is not fair, but that which pleascth.

There is no jollity but hath a smack of folly.

He that's long a giving knows not how to give.

The filth under the white snow the sun discovers.

Every one fastens where there is gain.

All feet tread not in one shoe.

Patience, time, and money accommodate all things.

For want of a nail the shoe is lost, for want of a shoe the horse is lost, for want of a horse the rider is lost.

Weight justly and sell dearly.

Little wealth little care.

Little journeys and good cost bring safe home.

Gluttony kills more than the sword.

When children stand quiet, they have done some ill.

A little and good fills the trencher.

A penny spared is twice got.

When a knave is in a plum-tree, he hath neither friend nor

Short boughs, long vintage. kin.

Health without money is half an ague.

If the wise erred not, it would go hard with fools.

Bear with evil, and expect good.

He that tells a secret, is another's servant.

If all fools wore white Caps, wo should seem a flock of geese.

Water, fire, and soldiers, quickly make room.

Pension never enriched a young man.

Under water, famine; under snow, bread.

The Lame goes as far as your staggerer.

He that loseth is Merchant, as well as ho that gains.

A jade cats as much as a good horse.

All things in their being are good for something.

One flower makes no garland.

A fair death honours the whole life.

One enemy is too much.

Living well is the best revenge.

One fool makes a hundred.

One pair of cars draws dry a hundred tongues.

A fool may throw a stone into a well, which a hundred wise

One slumber finds another. men cannot pull out.

On a good bargain think twice.

To a good spender God is the Treasurer.

A curst Cow hath short horns.

Music helps not the tooth-ache.

We cannot come to Honour under Coverlet.

Great pains quickly find ease.

To the counsel of fools a wooden bell.

The choleric man never wants woe.

Help thyself, and God will.help thee.

At the game's end we shall see who gains.

There arc many ways to fame.

Love is the true price of love.

Lovo rules his kingdom without a sword.

Lovo makes all hard hearts gentle.

Love makes a good eye squint.

Love asks faith, and faith firmness.

A sceptre is one thing, and a ladle another.

Great trees arc good for nothing but shade.

He commands enough that obeys a wise man.

Fair words make me look to my purse.

Though the fox run, the chicken hath wings.

lie plays well that wins.

You must strike in measure, when there arc many to strike

The shortest answer is doing. on one anvil.

It is a poor stake that cannot stand one year in the ground.

lie that commits a fault, thinks every one speaks of it. lie that is foolish in the fault, let him be wise in the punish

The blind cats many a fly. ment.

lie that can make a fire well, can end a quarrel

The tooth-ache is more case than to deal with ill people.

lie that would have what he hath not, should do what he

He that hath no good trade, it is to his loss. doth not.

The offender never pardons.

lie that lives not well one year, sorrows seven after.

Tic that hopes not for good, fears not evil.

lie that is angry at a feast, is rude. lie that mocks a cripple, ought to be whole.

When the tree is fallen, all go wi.h their hatchet.

He that hath horns in his bosom, let him not put them on

He that burns most, shines most. his head.

lie that trusts in a lie, shall perish in truth.

He that blows in the dust, fills his eyes with it.

Bells call others, but themselves enter not into the Church.

Of fair things, the Autumn is fair.

Giving is dead, restoring very sick.

A gift much expected is paid, not given.

Two ill meals make the third a glutton.

The Royal Crown cures not tho headache.

'Tis hard to be wretched, but worse to be known so.

It is better to be the head of a Lizard than the tail of a

A feather in hand is better than a bird in the air. Liou. Good and quickly seldom meet.

Happier are the hands compassed with iron, than a heart

Folly grows without-watering. with thoughts.

If the staff bo crooked, the shadow cannot be straight.

To take the nuts from the fire with the dog's foot.

He is a fool that makes a wedge of his fist.

Valour that parleys, is near yielding.

Thursday come, and the week is gone.

A flatterer's throat is an open sepulehre.

There is great force hidden in a sweet command.

The command of custom is great.

To have money is a fear, not to have it a grief.

The Cat sees not the mouse ever.

Little dogs start the hare, the great get her.

Willows arc weak, yet they bind other wood.

A good payer is master of another's purse.

The thread breaks where it is weakest.

Old men, when they scorn young, make much of death.

God is at the end, when we think he is furthest off it.

A good Judge conceives quickly, judges slowly.

Rivers need a spring.

He that contemplates, hath a day without night.

Give losers leave to talk.

Gaming, Women, and Wine, while they laugh, they make

Loss embraceth shame. men pine.

The nit man kuoweth not what the lean thinketh.

Wood half burnt is easily kindled.

The fish adores the bait.

He that goeth far hath many encounters.

Every bee's honey is sweet.

The slothful is the servant of the counters.

Wisdom hath one foot on land, and another on Sea.

The thought hath good legs, and the quill a good tongue.

A wise man needs not blush for changing his purpose.

The March sun raises, but dissolves not.

Time is the Rider that breaks youth.

The wine in the bottle doth not quench thirst.

The sight of a Man hath the force of a Lion.

An examined enterprise goes on boldly.

In every art it is good to have a master.

In every Country dogs bite.

In every Country the sun rises in the morning.

A noble plant suits not with a stubborn ground.

You may bring a horse to the river, but he will drink when and what he pleaseth. Before you make a friend, eat a bushel of salt with him.

Speak fitly, or be silent wisely.

Skill and confidence are an unconquered army.

I was taken by a morsel, says the fish.

A disarmed peace is weak.

The balance distinguished not between gold and lead.

The persuasion of the fortunate sways the doubtful.

To be beloved is above all bargains.

To deceive one's self is very easy.

The reasons of the poor weigh not.

Perverseness makes one squint-eyed.

The evening praises the day, and the morning a frost.

The table robs more than a thief.

When age is jocund, it makes sport for death.

True praise roots and spreads.

Fears are divided in the midst.

The soul needs few things, the body many.

Astrology is true, but the Astrologers cannot find it.

Tie it well, and let it go.

Empty vessels sound most.

Send not a Cat for Lard.

Foolish tongues talk by the dozen.

Love makes one fit for any work.

A pitiful mother makes a scald head.

An old Physician, and a young Lawyer.

Talk much, and err much, says the Spaniard.

Some make a conscience of spitting in the Church, yet rob

An idle head is a box for the wind. the Altar.

Show me a liar, and I will show thee a thief.

A bean in liberty is better than a comfit in prison.

Show a good man his error, and he turns it to a virtue;

None is born Master. but an ill, it doubles his fault.

None is offended but by himself.

None says his Garner is full.

In the husband wisdom, in the wife gentleness.

Nothing dries sooner than a tear.

In a leopard the spots are not observed.

Nothing lasts but the Church.

A wise man cares not for what he cannot have.

It is not good fishing before the net.

He cannot be virtuous that is not rigorous.

That which will not be spun, let it not come between the spindle and the distaff. "When my house burns, it is not good playing at Chess. No barber shaves so close but another finds work.

There is no great banquet, but some fares ill. A holy habit cleanseth not a foul soul. Forbear not sowing because of birds. Mention not a halter in the house of him that was hanged. Speak not of a dead man at the table. A hat is not made for one shower.

No sooner is a Temple built to God, but the Devil builds "Every one puts his fault on the Times, a Chapel hard by. You cannot make a windmill go with a pair of bellows. Every one is weary, the poor in seeking, the rich in keeping, Pardon all but thyself. the good in learning.

The escaped mouse ever feels the taste of the bait.

A little wind kindles, much puts out the fire.

Dry bread at home is better than roast meat abroad.

More have repented speech than silence.

The covetous spends more than the liberal.

Divine ashes are better than earthly meal.

Beauty draws more than oxen.

One father is more than a hundred Schoolmasters.

One eye of the master's sees more than ten of the servant's.

When God will punish, he will first take away the under

A little labour, much health. standing.

"When it thunders, the thief becomes honest.

The tree that God plants, no wind hurts it.

Knowledge is no burthen.

It is a bold mouse that nestles in the cat's ear.

If a good man thrive, all thrive with him.

If the mother had not been in the oven, she had never sought her daughter there. If great men would have care of little ones, both would last Long jesting was never good. long.

Though you see a Church-man ill, yet continue in the Church
Old praise dies, unless you feed it. still.

If things were to be done twice, all would be wise.

Had you the world on your Chessboard, you could not fill

Suffer and expect. all to your mind.

If fools should not fool it, they shall lose their season.

Love and business teach eloquence.

That which two will, takes effect.

He complains wrongfully on the sea, that twice suffers ship-

IIc is only bright that shines by himself. wreck.

A valiant man's look is more than a coward's sword.

The efTcct speaks, the tongue needs not.

Divine grace was never slow.

Reason lies between the spur and the bridle.

It is a proud horse that will not carry his own provender.

Three women make a market.

Three can hold their peace if two be away.

It is an ill counsel that hath no escape.

All our pomp the earth covers.

To whirl the eyes too much, shows a kite's brain.

Comparisons are odious.

All keys hang not on one girdle.

Great businesses turn on a littlo pin.

The wind in one's face makes one wiso.

All the arms of England will not arm fear.

One sword keeps another in the sheath.

Be what thou wouldst seem to be.

Let all live as they would die.

A gentle heart is tied with an easy thread.

Sweet discourse makes short days and nights.

God provides for him that trustcth.

He that will not have peace, God gives him war.

To him that Mill, ways arc not wanting.

To a great night, a great Lanthorn.

To a child all weather is cold.

"Where there is peace, God is.

None is so wise, but the fool overtakes him.

Fools give to please all but their own.

Prosperity lets go the bridle.

The Friar preached against stealing, and had a goose in his

To be too busy gets contempt. sleeve.

February makes a bridge, and March breaks it.

The best smell is bread, the best savour salt, the best lovo

A horse stumbles that hath four legs. that of children.

That is tho best gown that goes up and down tho house.

The Market is the best Garden.

The first dish pleascth all.

Tho higher tho Ape goes, the mora he shows his tail.

Night is tho mother of Councils.

God's Mill grinds slow, but sure.

Every one thinks his sack heaviest.

Drought never brought dearth.

All complain.

Gamesters and race-horses never last long.

It is a poor sport that is not worth the candle.

lie that is fallen cannot help him that is down.

Every one is witty for his own purpose

A little let lets an ill workman.

Good workmen arc seldom rich.

By doing nothing we learn to do ill.

A great dowry is a bed full of brambles.

No profit to honour, no honour to Religion.

Every sin brings its punishment with it.

Of him that speaks ill, consider the life more than tlic word.

You cannot hide an eel in a sack.

Give not Saint *Peter* so much, to leave Saint *Paul* nothing.

You cannot flay a stone.

The chief disease that reigns this year is folly.

A sleepy master makes his servant a Lout.

Better speak truth rudely, than lie covertly.

He that fears leaves, let him not go into the wood.

One foot is better than two crutches.

Neither praise nor dispraise thyself, thy actions serve the

Better suffer ill, than do ill. turn.

The constancy of the benefit of the year in their seasons

Soft and fair goes far. argues a Deity.

Praise none too much, for all arc fickle.

It is absurd to warm one in his armour.

Lawsuits consume time, and money, and rest, and friends.

Nature draws more than ten teams.

He that hath a wife and children, wants not business.

A ship and a woman arc ever repairing.

He that fears death, lives not.

lie that pities.another, remembers himself.' lie that doth what he should not, shall feel what ho would

He that marries for wealth, sells his liberty. not.

He that once hits, is ever bendiug.

lie that serves, must serve. lie that lends, gives. lie that prcachcth, givcth alms.

He that cockers his child, provides for his enemy.

A pitiful look asks enough.

"Who will sell the cow, must say tho word.

Service is no inheritance.

The faulty stands on his guard.

A kinsman, a friend, or whom you entreat, take not to serve you, if you will be served neatly.

At Court, every one for himself.

To a crafty man, a crafty and a half, lie that is thrown, would ever wrestle, lie that serves well, needs not ask hia wages.

Fair language grates not tho tongue.

A good heart cannot lie.

Good swimmers at length arc drowned.

Good land, evil way.

In doing wo learn.

It is good walking with a horse in one's hand.

God, and Parents, and our Master, can never bo requited.

An ill deed cannot bring honour.

A small heart hath small desires.

All arc not merry that dance lightly.

Courtesy on one sido only, lasts not long.

"Wine-Counsels seldom prosper.

Weening is not measure.

The best of the sport is to do the deed, and say nothing.

If thou thyself canst do it, attend no other's help or hand.

Of a little thing, a little displeaseth.

God keep me from four houses, a Usurer's, a Tavern, a

No warms too near that burns. Spital, and a Prison.

In a hundred ells of contention, there is not an inch of love.

Do what thou oughtest, and come what come can.

Hunger makes dinners, pastime suppers.

In a long journey straw weighs.

Women laugh when they can, and weep when they will.

War is death's feast.

Sot good against evil.

He that brings good news knocks hard.

Beat the Dog before the Lion.

Haste comes not alone.

You must lose a fly to catch a trout.

Better a snotty child than his nose wiped off.

lie is not free that draws his chain.

He goes not out of his way that goes to a good inn.

There comes nought out of the sack, but what was there.

A little given seasonably, excuses a great gift.

He looks not well to himself that looks not ever.

He thinks not well, that thinks not again.

Religion, Credit, and the Eye are not to be touched.

The tongue is not steel, yet it cuts.

A white wall is the paper of a fool.

They talk of Christmas so long, that it comes.

That is gold which is worth gold.

It is good tying the sack before it be full.

Words arc women, deeds arc men.

Poverty is no sin.

A stone in a well is not lost.

Ho can give little to his servant that licks his knife.

Promising is the eve of giving.

He that keeps his own, makes war.

The wolf must die in his own skin.

Goods arc theirs that enjoy them.

He that sends a fool, expects one.

He that can stay, obtains.

lie that gains well and spends well, needs no account book.

He that endures, is not overcome.

He that gives all before he dies, provides to suffer.

He that talks much of his happiness, summons grief.

He that loves the tree, loves the branch.

Who hastens a glutton, chokes him.

Who praiseth Saint *Peter,* doth not blame Saint *Paul.*

He that hath not the craft, let him shut up shop.

He that knows nothing, doubts nothing.

Green wood makes a hot fire.

He that marries late, marries ill.

He that passeth a winter's day, escapes an enemy.

The rich knows not who is his friend.

A morning Sun, and a Wine-bred child, and a Latin-bred woman, seldom end well.

To a close shorn sheep, God gives wind by measure.

A pleasure long expected, is dear enough sold.

A poor man's cow dies, a rich man's child.

The cow knows not what her tail is worth till she have lost it.

Choose a horse made, and a wife to make.

It is an ill air where we gain nothing.

He hath not lived, that lives not after death.

So many men in court, and so many strangers.

He quits his place well, that leaves his friend here.

That which sufficeth is not little.

Good news may be told at any time, but ill in the morning,

lie that would be a Gentleman, let him go to an assault.

Who pays the Physician, does the cure.

None knows the weight of another's burthen.

Every one hath a fool in his sleeve.

One hour's sleep before midnight is worth three after.

In a retreat the lame arc foremost.

It is more pain to do nothing than something.

Amongst good men two men suffice.

There needs a long time to know the world's pulse.

The offspring of those that arc very young, or very old, lasts

A tyrant is most tyrant to himself. not.

Too much taking heed is loss.

Craft against craft, makes no living.

The Reverend are ever before.

Franco is a meadow that cuts thrice a year.

It is easier to build two chimneys, than to maintain one.

The Court hath no Almanack.

He that will enter into Paradise, must have a good key.

When you enter into a house, leave the anger ever at the

He hath no leisure who useth it not. door.

It is a wicked thing to make a dearth one's garner.

He that deals in the world needs four sieves.

Take heed of an ox before, of a horse behind, of a monk on

The year doth nothing else but open and shut. all sides.

The ignorant hath an Eagle's wings and an Owl's eyes.

There arc more Physicians in health than drunkards.

The wife is the key of the house.

The Law is not the same at morning and at night.

War and Physic arc governed by the eye.

Half the world knows not how the other half lies.

Death keeps no Calendar.

Ships fear fire more than water.

The least foolish is wise.

The chief box of health is time.

Silks and Satins put out the fire in the chimney.

The first blow is as much as two.

The life of man is a winter way.

The way is an ill neighbour.

An old man's staff is the rapper of death's door.

Life is half spent, before we know what it is.

The singing man keeps his shop in his throat.

The body is more dressed than the soul.

The body is sooner dressed than the soul.

The Physician owes all to the patient, but the patient owes nothing to him but a little money.

The little cannot be great, unless ho devour many.

The Choleric drinks, the Melancholic eats, the Phlegmatic
Time undermines us. sleeps.

The Apothecary's mortar spoils the lutcr's music.

Conversation makes one what ho is.

The deaf gains the injury.

Years know more than books.

Wine is a turn-coat (first a friend, then an enemy).

"Wine ever pays for his lodging.

Wine makes all sorts of creatures at table.

Wine that cost nothing is digested before it be drunk.

Trees cat but once.

Armour is light at table.

Good horses make short miles.

Castles arc Forests of stones.

The dainties of the great arc the tears of tho poor.

Parsons arc souls' wagoners.

Children when they are little make parents fools, when they
arc great they make them mad.

The Master absent, and the houso dead.

Dogs arc fine in the field.

Sins are not known till they be acted.

Thorns whiten, yet do nothing.

All arc presumed good till they arc found in a fault.

The great put the little on tho hook.

The great would have none great, and the little all little.

The Italians are wise before the deed, tho Germans in the
deed, the French after the deed. Every mile is two in winter.

Spectacles arc death's Arquebuse.

Lawyers' houses arc built on the heads of fools.

.The house is a fine house when good folks are within.

The best bred have the best portion.

The first and last frosts are the worst, (jifts enter every where without a wim-

ble.

Princes have no way.

Knowledge makes one laugh, but wealth makes one dance.

The Citizen is at his business before he rise.

The eyes have one language every where.

It is better to have wings than horns.

Better be a fool than a knave.

Count not four, except you have them in a wallet.

To live peaceably with all, breeds good blood.

You may be on land, yet not in a garden.

You cannot make the fire so low, but it will get out.

Wc know not who lives or dies.

An ox is taken by the horns, and a man by the tongue.

Many things arc lost for want of asking.

No Church-yard is so handsome, that a man would desiro
straight to be buried there.

Cities arc taken by the cars.

Once a year a man may say, On his conscience.

Wc leave more to do when wc die, than wc have done.

With customs wc live well, but laws undo us.

To speak of a Usurer at the table, mars the wine.

Pains to get, care to keep, fear to lose.

For a morning rain, leave not your journey.

One fair day in winter makes not birds merry.

He that learns a trade, hath a purchase made.

When all men have what belongs to them, it cannot be much.

Though God take the sun out of the heaven, yet we must
have patience. When a mau sleeps, his head is in his stomach.

x

When God is made the master of a family, he orders the dis

When one is on horseback, he knows all things. orderly.

When a Lackey comes to hell's door, tho Devils lock the

He that is at ease, seeks dainties. gates.

He that hath charge of souls, transports them not in bundles.

Ho that tells his wife news, is but newly married.

He that is in a town in May loscth his Spring.

lie that is in a Tavern, thinks ho is in a vine-garden.

He that praiseth himself, spattcreth himself.

He that is surprised with the first frost, feels it all the winter lie that is a master, must servo (another). after.

Ilea beast doth die, that hath dono no good to his country.

lie that follows the Lord, hopes to go before. lie that dies without tho company of good men, puts not himself into a good way. "Who hath no haste in his business, mountains to him seem Who hath no head, needs no heart. valleys.

Speak not of my debts, unless you mean to pay thom.

lie that is not in tho wars, is not out of danger,

He that gives mo small gifts, would havo mo live.

Ho that is his own Counsellor, knows nothing sure but what

He that hath lands, hath quarrels. (ho hath laid out.

He that goes to bed thirsty, riscth healthy.

Who will make a door of gold, must knock a nail every day.

A trade is better than service.

He that lives in hope, danccth without musie.

To review one's store is to mow twice.

Saint *Luko* was a Saint and a Physician, yet is dead.

Without business, debauchery.

Without danger we cannot get beyond danger.

Health and sickness surely arc men's double enemies.

If gold knew what gold is, gold would get gold, I wis.

Little losses amaze, great tame.

Choose none for thy servant who hath served thy betters.

Service without reward is punishment.

If tho husband be not at home, there is nobody.

An oath that is not to bo made, is not to be kept.

Tiio eye is bigger than tho belly.

If you would bo at case, all tho world is not.

Were it not for the bono in tho leg, all tho world would turn

Carpenters (to mako thcin crutches). If you must fly, fly well. All that shakes falls not. All beasts of prey arc strong, or treacherous. If the brain sows not corn, it plants thistles. A man well mounted is ever Cholerie. Every one is a master and servant. A piece of a Church-yard fits every body. One mouth doth nothing without another. A master of straw cats a servant of steel. An old cat sports not with her prey. A woman conceals what she knows not. lie that wipes tho child's nose, kisscth the mother's cheek. Gentility is nothing but Ancient Riches. To go where the King goes afoot; i. c, to the stool. To go upon the Franciscans' Hackney; i. e. , on foot. *Amicus* was taken by the Fox, and retaken by the Lion. After Death the Doctor. Ready money is a ready Medicine. It is the Philosophy of the DistafF. It is a sheep of *Beery,* it is marked on the nose: applied to those that have a blow. To build castles in Spain. An Idle youth, a needy Age. Silk doth quench the fire in the Kitchen. The words ending in *ique,* do mock the Physician; as Hcc tique, Paralytique, Apoplectique, Lcthargique.

Tho proverbs which follow were »dJcd to the second edition. lie that trusts much Obliges much, says the Spaniard. lie that thinks amiss, concludes worse. A man would live in Italy (a place of pleasure), but he would choose to die in Spain, where they say the Catholic

Religion is professed with greatest strictness. Whatsoever was the father of a disease, an ill diet was tho Frenzy, Heresy, and Jealousy, seldom cured. mother.

There is no heat of affection but is joined with some idleness of brain, says tho Spaniard.

The War is not done so long as my Enemy lives.

Some evils arc cured by contempt.

Tower seldom grows old at Court.

Danger itself the best remedy for danger.

Favour will as surely perish as life.

Fear the Beadle of tho Law.

For the same man to be a heretic and a good subject, is iu-

Ilcresy is the school of pride. compossible.

Heresy may be easier kept out than shook off.

Infants' manners are moulded more by the example of

Parents, than by stars at their nativities. They favour learning whose actions arc worthy of a learned

Modesty sets off one newly come to honour. pen.

No naked man is sought after to be rifled.

There is no such conquering weapon as the necessity of con-

Nothing secure unless suspected. quering.

No tic can oblige the perfidious.

Spies arc the cars and eyes of Princes.

The life of spies is to know, not be known.

Religion a stalking-horse to shoot other fowl.

It is a dangerous fire begins in the bed straw.

Covctousness breaks the bag.

Fear keeps and looks to the vineyard, and not the owner.

The noise is greater than the nuts.

Two sparrows.on one Ear of Corn make an ill agreement.

The world is now-a-days, God save the Conqueror.

Unsound minds, like unsound Bodies, if you feed, you poison.

Not only ought fortune to be pictured on a wheel, but every

thing else in this world. All covet, all lose.

Better is one *Accipe,* than twice to say, *Dabo tibi.*

An Ass endures his burden, but not more than his burden.

Threatened men eat bread, says the Spaniard.

The beads in the Hand, and the Devil in Capuch; or, cape
of the cloak.

He that will do thec a good turn, cither

he will be gone or

I escaped the Thunder, and fell into the Lightning. die.

A man of a great memory without learning, hath a rock and

a spindle, and no staff to spin. The death of wolves is the safety of the sheep. lie that is once born, once must die.

He that hath but one eye, must be afraid to lose it.

He that makes himself a sheep, shall be eat by the wolf.

lie that steals an egg, will steal an ox. lie that will be surety, shall pay.

He that is afraid of leaves, goes not to the wood.

In the mouth of a bad dog falls often a good bone.

Those that God loves, do not live long.

Still fishcth he that catchcth one.

All flesh is not venison.

A City that parleys is half gotten.

A dead bee makcth no honey.

An old dog barks not in vain.

They that hold the greatest farms, pay the least rent: applied to rich men that are unthankful to God.

Old Camels carry young Camels' skins to the market.

He that hath time and looks for better time, time comes that he repents himself of time.

Words and feathers the wind carries away.

Of a pig's tail you can never make a good shaft.

Tho Bath of the Blackamoor hath sworn not to whiten.

To a greedy eating horse a short halter.

The Devil divides the world between Atheism and Supersti

Such a Saint, such an offering. tion.

"We do it soon enough, if that we do be well.

Cruelty is more cruel, if we defer the pain.

What one day gives us, another takes away from us.

To seek in a Sheep five feet when there arc but four.

A scabbed horse cannot abide the comb.

God strikes with his finger, and not

with all his arm.

God gives his wrath by weight, and without weight his mercy.

Of a new Prince, new bondage.

Fortune to one is Mother, to another is Step-mother.

There is no man, though never so little, but sometimes he

New things arc fair. can hurt.

The horse that draws after him his halter, is not altogether

No love is foul, nor prison fair. escaped.

We must recoil a little, to the end we may leap tho better.

No day so clear, but hath dark clouds.

No hair so small, but hath his shadow.

A wolf will never make war against another wolf.

We must love, as looking one day to hate.

It is good to have some friends both in heaven and hell.

It is very hard to shave an egg.

It is good to hold the ass by the bridle.

The healthful man can give counsel to tho sick.

The death of a young wolf doth never come too soon.

Tho rage of a wild boar is able to spoil more than one wood.

Virtue flies from the heart of a Mercenary man.

The wolf cats oft of the sheep that hath been warned.

The mouso that hath but one hole is quickly taken.

To play at Chess when the house is on fire.

Tho itch of disputing is the scab of the Church.

Follow not truth too near the heels, lest it dash out thy teeth.

Either wealth is much increased, or moderation is much

When war begins, then hell opencth. decayed.

Say to pleasure, Gentle *Eve,* I will none of your apple.

There is a remedy for every thing, could men find it.

There is an hour wherein a man might be happy all his life,

could he find it.

Great Fortune brings with it Great misfortune.

A fair day in winter is the mother of a storm.

Woe bo to him that reads but one book. Tithe, and be rich.

The wrath of a mighty man, and the tumult of the

Mad folks in a narrow place. people.

Credit decayed, and people that have nothing.

A young wench, a prophetess, and a Latin-bred woman.

A person marked,.and a Widow thrice married.

Foul dirty ways, and long sickness.

Wind that comes in at a hole, and a reconciled Enemy.

A Step-mother; the very name of her sufficeth. Critics arc like brushcrs of Noblemen's clothes. He is a great Necromancer, for he asks counsel of the

Dead: *i. e.,* books. A man is known to be mortal by two things, Sleep and Princes are venison in Heaven. Lust.

Love without end, hath no end, says the Spaniard: meaning, if it were not begun on particular ends, it would last. Stay a while, that we may make an end

the sooner. Presents of love fear not to be ill taken of strangers. To seek these things is lost labour: Geese in an oil pot, fat Hogs among Jews, and Wine in a fishing net. Some men plant an opinion they seem to eradicate. The Philosophy of Princes is to dive into the Secrets of men, leaving the secrets of nature to those that have spare time.

States have their conversions and periods as well as natural Great deservers grow Intolerable presumers. bodies.

The love of money and the love of learning rarely meetTrust no friend with that you need, fear him if he were your enemy. Some had rather lose their friend than their Jest. Marry your daughters betimes, less they marry themselves. Soldiers in peace are like chimneys in summer. Here is a talk of the Turk and the Pope, but my next neighbour doth me more harm than cither of them both. Civil Wars of *France* made a million of Atheists, and thirty thousand Witches. Wo Bachelors laugh and show our teeth, but you married men laugh till your hearts ache. The Devil never assails a man except he find him either void of knowledge, or of the fear of God. There is nobody will go to hell for company. Much money makes a Country poor, for it sets a dearer price upon every thing. The virtue of a coward is suspicion. A man's destiny is always dark. Every man's censure is first moulded in his own nature. Money wants no followers. Your thoughts close, and your countenance loose. Whatever is made by the hand of man, by the hand of man may be overturned.

CPSIA information can be obtained at www.ICGtesting.com
Printed in the USA
BVOW01s1027240914

368160BV00020B/770/P

9 781230 250700